Creative Kids

Simple Cooking Fun

Cooking & Stories

Written by

Sharon Draznin

Teacher Created Materials, Inc.

Teacher Created Materials, Inc.
6421 Industry Way
Westminster, CA 92683
www.teachercreated.com
2004 Teacher Created Materials, Inc.

Made in the U.S.A.

ISBN #0-7439-3197-1

Editor:

Stephanie Buehler, M.P.W., M.A.

Cover Art:

Tony Carrillo

Illustrator:

Barb Lorseyedi

Table of Contents

Table of Contents *(cont.)*

Table of Contents *(cont.)*

Introduction

Welcome to Simple Cooking Fun!

The delicious recipes in this 160-page book will provide you and your children with hours of cooking and eating fun.

In addition to spending treasured moments with your child, the activities in this book will enhance many skills. Don't be surprised if your child's confidence and self-esteem increase as he or she "learns by doing."

More Than a Cookbook

The cooking projects provide a highly motivating, real-life application for learning. As your child experiences *Simple Cooking Fun*, his or her skills in reading, mathematics, social studies, science, and fine arts will also be enriched. Here's how!

- In order to cook successfully, children must be able to read and comprehend the recipe even if they are only "reading" the pictures. The step-by-step format which cooking requires helps children learn how to think sequentially and develop recall skills. Often, new vocabulary words are introduced in recipes, particularly as children encounter the words for various cooking procedures.

- Math skills required in cooking include using money to buy ingredients, measuring, weighing, counting, sorting, estimating, using fractions, basic arithmetic operations (addition, subtraction, multiplication, and division), using a clock or timer, one-to-one correspondence, patterning, recognizing shapes, and graphing favorite recipes and foods.

More Than a Cookbook (cont.)

- When your child cuts an apple into eight parts, names each part as one-eighth, calls each eighth a wedge and then cooks the pieces for ten minutes as part of the applesauce-making process there is a great deal of math going on!

- Your child will also broaden his or her awareness of the community and the world as he or she learns about where foods come from and begins to understand how foods are grown and transported. When shopping for ingredients, children learn about stores in their community.

- Children also come to realize the importance of the adults in their own lives who provide them with food. They participate in sharing as they distribute the "snacks" they have made among friends and/or family. Children learn about foods from other countries as well as foods from their own backgrounds as they participate in the literature and cooking experiences provided in this book. Finally, children also learn and practice social skills when participating in cooking. They practice saying "please" and "thank-you" or "no, thank-you." They learn to wait until everyone is served before beginning to eat. They practice asking for second helpings politely.

- Children experience "the science of cooking" as they watch liquids poured into a measuring cup take the shape of that container. They begin to understand how foods grow, where they come from, seasonal aspects of certain foods (watermelon, for example) and which parts of plants we consider edible. They realize how our bodies use food and the effects of various foods on the body (nutrition).

More Than a Cookbook *(cont.)*

- The senses are involved in food preparation since sight, smell, taste, and texture are closely related to cooking experience's. Children can actually see how foods change when heat or cold is applied. They participate in combining single ingredients which then become an entirely different product which can no longer be broken down into its components.

- As your child observes the cooking process, he or she will probably ask questions. If your child makes a mistake, take the opportunity to talk about what might have gone wrong and how the problem can be corrected. You will be helping your child think scientifically!

- Food storage and safety in food handling and in using kitchen equipment are additional aspects of cooking which can be addressed through the cooking experience.

- Finally, cooking and fine arts connect as students exercise creativity in food preparation and presentation, write illustrated recipes and cooking stories, appreciate the colors of various foods and serve food in an attractive way, perhaps using decorative place settings.

Cooking encourages young children to try new foods, helps them become familiar with various ingredients and teaches processes and techniques. Children love eating what they've made. Cooking makes learning both fun and memorable. It offers something to benefit every participant.

How to Use This Book

Simple Cooking Fun was written for use by both parents and teachers of kindergarten through third graders and for other group leaders such as scouts or youth groups. The format has been designed for clarity and ease of use. The literature selections are readily available from bookstores, book clubs, school or community libraries, classrooms, or home collection.

Each book selection is presented in seven sections:

1. **Before You Cook** provides a summary of the literature selection and sets the scene.

2. **From The Store** lists items to be purchased at the grocery store.

3. **From The Pantry** lists "on hand" staples which are usually bought in bulk and are available in most people's kitchens, such as flour, sugar, salt, etc.

4. **Utensils To Gather** lists all the tools, pots, and pans needed to prepare the recipe.

5. **The Recipe** section provides the actual recipe and preparation procedure in a step-by-step format.

6. **Extra Helping** suggests extended activities related to the literature selection. These activities may be completed at home, at school, or at the library.

7. **Books For Dessert** lists related literature selections.

Before You Get Started

Discuss the rules on this page before you attempt any recipes with children. Group leaders may wish to reproduce and display rules on poster board.

Before You Cook

1. Wash your hands.
2. Put on an apron.
3. Read the recipe.
4. Gather the utensils and ingredients.
5. Follow the recipe steps in order.
6. Clean up as you go.

After You Cook

1. Be sure all appliances are turned off and unplugged.
2. Wash and dry all utensils.
3. Put everything away.
4. Leave everything neat and clean.

Rules for Cooking Safely

1. Let the adult help with sharp knives and hot appliances.
2. Use a cutting board to chop foods. Cut away from the body.
3. Use potholders for hot pots and pans. Keep handles turned in towards stove.
4. Turn off and unplug appliances when finished using them.
5. Wipe up spills when they happen.
6. Roll up long sleeves.
7. Tie back long hair.
8. Cover your mouth when you sneeze or cough, and then wash your hands again.
9. Do not put food in your mouth while cooking.
10. Use a step stool or other steady surface to raise you to the proper height for work or to look for supplies.

Group Cooking Experiences

If you are a classroom teacher or youth group leader, this book will work well for your group cooking experiences. You can easily make cooking part of your activity program. Recipes are best completed in groups of six to eight children.

Before the designated cooking day, review the literature selection and the recipe. Use the shopping guide and utensils list to help you complete the parent letter included on page 151. Make copies of the letter to be sent home. You will also need to either make one copy of the recipe for each group of children or copy the recipe on a large sheet of tagboard or an overhead transparency to display in the cooking area. If you will need additional adult supervision on cooking day, seek out a parent volunteer.

On cooking day, share the literature selection and the recipe with the group. Discuss any special instructions and review safety procedures. If you have not done so in advance, have your adult helper prepare the cooking area.

Please note how portions are to be divided. Recipes like applesauce or rice pudding are to be cooked in large batches, then shared. Recipes like cornbread and whole wheat bread are to be cut into the correct number of portions. Finally, recipes like English Muffin Pizza and Ants on a Log are made and served in individual portions.

You may wish to post a copy of the recipe and allow children to hand-copy it. This gives children the opportunity to share the recipe with their friends or families. Each recipe can be sent home individually or recipes can be collected and bound into a cookbook. The cookbook could then be used as a gift for someone special.

Math in the Kitchen

Equivalent Measures

3 teaspoons = 1 tablespoon
4 tablespoons = ¼ cup
5 ⅓ tablespoons = ⅓ cup
8 tablespoons = ½ cup
12 tablespoons = ¾ cup
16 tablespoons = 1
   cup or ½ pint or 8 ounces
2 cups = 1 pint or 16 ounces
4 cups = 1 quart, or roughly, 1 liter
4 quarts = 1 gallon
1 fluid ounce = 2 tablespoons
½ stick butter or margarine = ¼ cup
1 stick butter or margarine
   = ½ cup or ¼ pound
2 sticks butter or margarine = 1 cup
   or ½ pound
   4 sticks butter or margarine
   = 2 cups or one pound

Metric Conversions

United States Customary measurement is used throughout this book. For metric conversions, use the information below to find equivalent measurements.

1 teaspoon = 5 milliliters
1 tablespoon = 15 milliliters
¼ cup = 60 milliliters
⅓ cup = 80 milliliters
½ cup = 125 milliliters
¾ cup = 185 milliliters
1 cup = 250 milliliters

Oven Temperatures

The oven temperature for all recipes in this book is measured in Fahrenheit degrees. To convert Fahrenheit degrees to Celsius, subtract 32 degrees and multiply by ⅝. To convert Celsius degrees to Fahrenheit, multiply by ⅝ and add 32 degrees—or use the handy chart below!

Fahrenheit	Celsius
250-275	125-135
300-325	150-165
350-275	175-190
400-425	205-220
450-475	230-245

Linear Measures

Refer to the following measurements for any linear metric conversion information you may need in this book.

1" = 2.54 cm   5" = 25 cm   11" = 28 cm
2" = 5 cm   8" = 20 cm   12" = 30 cm
2 ½" = 6.4 cm   8 ½" = 22 cm   14 " = 36 cm
3" = 8 cm   9" = 23 cm   17" = 43 cm

A Cooking Word List for Children

Action Words

add
measure
spread
bake
mix
sprinkle
blend
pour
stir
chop
refrigerate
toss
combine
roll
whip
cut
scrape
grease
shake
knead
slice

Nouns

ingredients
scissors
sponge
measuring spoons
spatula
soap
food processor
measuring cups
bowl
chopping board
rolling pin
beater
knife
muffin tin
cookie sheet
peeler
loaf pan
hot plate
scraper
toaster oven
mixer
blender
sauce pan
whisk
grater
frying pan
colander

Kitchen Tools

fork

spatula

measuring cups

cookie sheet

Kitchen Tools *(cont.)*

spatula

oven mitts

knife

mixing bowl

wire whisk

rolling pin

colander

grater

wooden mixing spoon

hot plate

Cooking Supplies

Check off the items you have. Then it will be easy to see what is still needed.

Kitchen Ware

- ❏ baking pans
- ❏ can opener
- ❏ cookie sheets
- ❏ knives
- ❏ measuring cups
- ❏ measuring spoons
- ❏ mixing bowls
- ❏ mixing spoons
- ❏ muffin tins
- ❏ peeler
- ❏ soup pot
- ❏ spatula
- ❏ storage containers
- ❏ strainer or colander

Small Appliances

- ❏ blender
- ❏ crock pot
- ❏ electric frying pan
- ❏ food processor
- ❏ hot plate

Pantry Staples

- ❏ baking powder
- ❏ baking soda
- ❏ brown sugar
- ❏ chocolate chips
- ❏ cinnamon
- ❏ flour
- ❏ powdered sugar
- ❏ raisins
- ❏ salt
- ❏ sugar
- ❏ vanilla
- ❏ peanut butter

Miscellany

- ❏ aluminum foil
- ❏ dish towels
- ❏ dish soap
- ❏ napkins
- ❏ pot holders
- ❏ paper muffin liners
- ❏ paper plates, bowls, cups
- ❏ paper towels
- ❏ plastic eating utensils
- ❏ plastic wrap
- ❏ waxed paper
- ❏ vegetable oil

Creating a Classroom or Youth Group Cooking Center

Set Up

If possible, set up your cooking center close to a sink and next to shelves, cabinets, or other storage areas. Place staples such as flour, sugar, and salt in tightly sealed containers. A cart can provide useful storage space and has the added advantage of being mobile, therefore permitting you to easily share supplies with other classes or groups. An extra-large plastic container with a lid can also provide necessary storage space for a cooking center and keep everything in reach.

Supplies

Be creative when gathering basic cooking supplies.

- Parents may wish to donate items, both food and utensils.
- Shop at garage sales and second hand stores for inexpensive appliances and utensils. (You may want to have them checked by a handy person before plugging them in.)
- Have a "kitchen shower" and invite parents. Create a "wish list" in the form of a colorful invitation and send it home with students or group participants; on the day of the shower, serve cookies and lemonade prepared by the students.
- Perhaps the PTA or similar organization will assist you with donations of money, appliances, or utensils.
- Recycle aluminum cans to generate cash which can be used for purchases.
- Have your class hold a bake sale or other fundraiser for the school in order to raise money for necessary cooking center supplies.

Setting the Table

This is how you might set the table for yourself, your family, and your friends.

To make the table look really special, you might want to make some woven placemats. Here are the directions:

For each placemat you will need:

- 12" x 18" construction paper
- 12" x 18" construction paper cut into 1" wide strips
  (Choose contrasting colors or your two favorite colors for the paper.)
- scissors
- glue

Cut slits in the 12" x 18" piece of construction paper. Weave the strips cut from the other piece of construction paper through the slits: over, under, over, under, etc. Glue the ends down.

Note: The finished placemats can be laminated or covered with clear contact paper. Then they can be wiped off after a meal and reused.

The Food Pyramid

The Food Guide Pyramid was created by the United States Department of Agriculture (USDA) as a way of presenting our government's latest guidelines for a healthy diet. The following pyramid shows what a daily balanced diet looks like.

Key

● Fat (naturally occurring and added)

▼ Sugars (added)

These symbols show that fat and added sugars come mostly from fats, oils, and sweets, but can be part of or added to foods from the food groups as well.

A Guide to Daily Food Choices

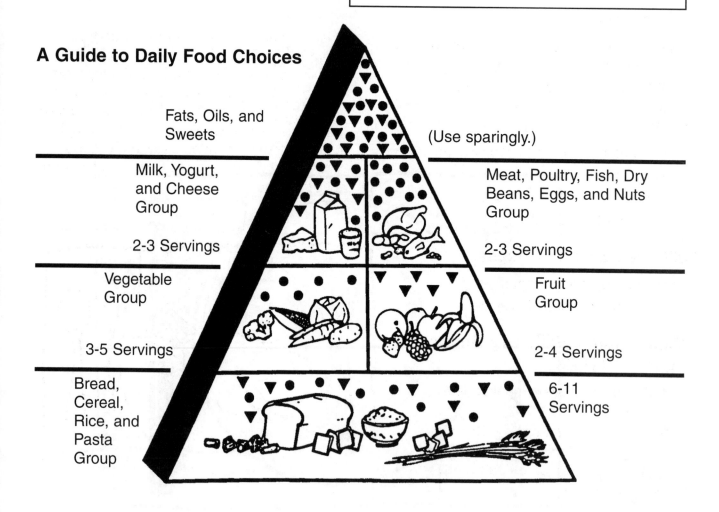

Fats, Oils, and Sweets

(Use sparingly.)

Milk, Yogurt, and Cheese Group

2-3 Servings

Meat, Poultry, Fish, Dry Beans, Eggs, and Nuts Group

2-3 Servings

Vegetable Group

3-5 Servings

Fruit Group

2-4 Servings

Bread, Cereal, Rice, and Pasta Group

6-11 Servings

The Food Pyramid *(cont.)*

Serving Sizes

To help you determine the amount of food that makes up a serving size, the U.S. Department of Agriculture has established these guidelines.

Bread and Cereals, Rice and Pasta

- 1 slice of bread
- ½ cup of cooked rice or pasta
- ½ cup of cooked cereal
- 1 ounce of ready-to-eat cereal

Vegetables

- ½ cup of chopped raw or cooked vegetables
- 1 cup of leafy raw vegetables

Fruits

- 1 piece of fruit or melon wedge
- ¾ cup of juice
- ½ cup of canned fruit
- ¼ cup of dried fruit

Milk, Yogurt, and Cheese

- 1 cup of milk or yogurt
- 1 ½ to 2 ounces of cheese

Meat, Poultry, Fish, Dry Beans, Eggs, and Nuts

- 2 ½ to 3 ounces of cooked lean meat, poultry, or fish
- (Count ½ cup of cooked beans, or 1 egg, or 2 tablespoons of peanut butter as 1 ounce of lean meat— about ⅓ serving.)

Fats, Oils, and Sweets

Limit calories from these, especially if you need to lose weight.

The amount you eat may be more than one serving. For example, a dinner portion of spaghetti would count as two or three servings of pasta.

It is felt that grains and foods made from them should be the foundation of our diet, providing about 40% of our total daily food intake, whereas fats and sweets should be used sparingly. Most nutrition experts agree that a diet rich in whole grains and complex carbohydrates provides us with the good health and vigor we need to lead active and fulfilling lives.

Apron Patterns

To create your own apron, choose one of the following styles. Gather the materials and follow the directions below. Pattern details for each apron style can be found on pages 23 and 24.

Style 1

Materials

- ½ yard cloth
- 2 yards cotton cording or ribbon
- newspaper
- ruler
- scissors
- needle and thread or sewing machine

Directions

Fold a sheet of newspaper and measure according to the diagram shown. Use the newspaper pattern to cut out the fabric. Hem the edges. Fold side A over 1 ½ inches. Do the same for side B. Sew each in ¼ inch from the cut edge. Thread cording or ribbon through A and B to form ties and neck loop. Knot the ends of the cording.

Style 2

Materials

- kitchen towel or a 30" x 15" piece of fabric
- 1 yard cotton cording or ribbon
- needle and thread or sewing machine

Directions

If using a towel, fold one side down 1 ½ inch. Sew ¼ inch in from the edge. Push the cording or ribbon through from A to B to form tie. Knot the ends of each tie.

If using fabric, hem all edges. Fold a 30 inch edge down 1 inch and sew. Push cording or ribbon through from A to B. Knot the ends of each tie.

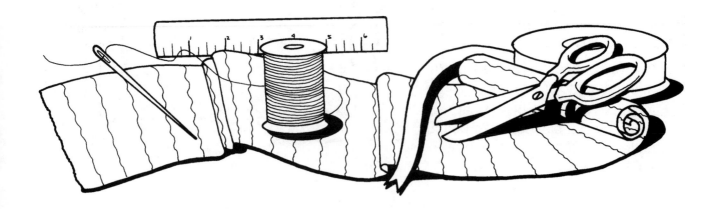

Style 1

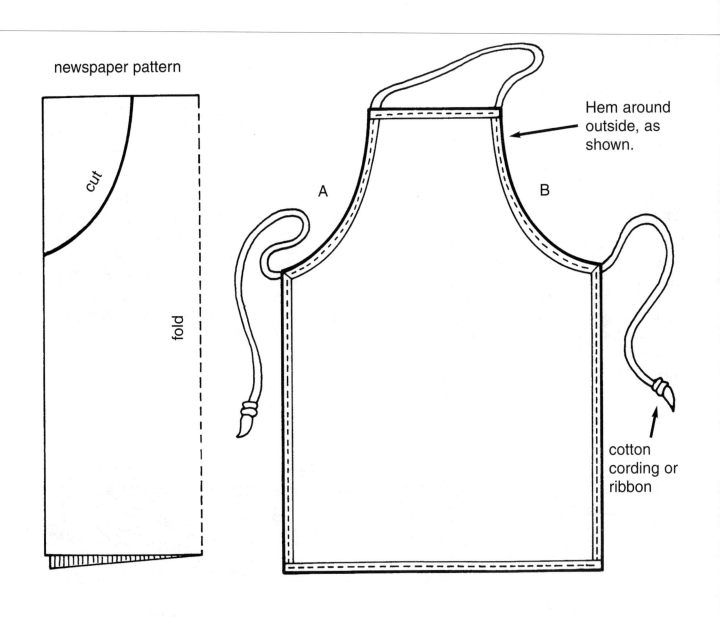

newspaper pattern

cut

fold

Hem around outside, as shown.

A

B

cotton cording or ribbon

Style 2

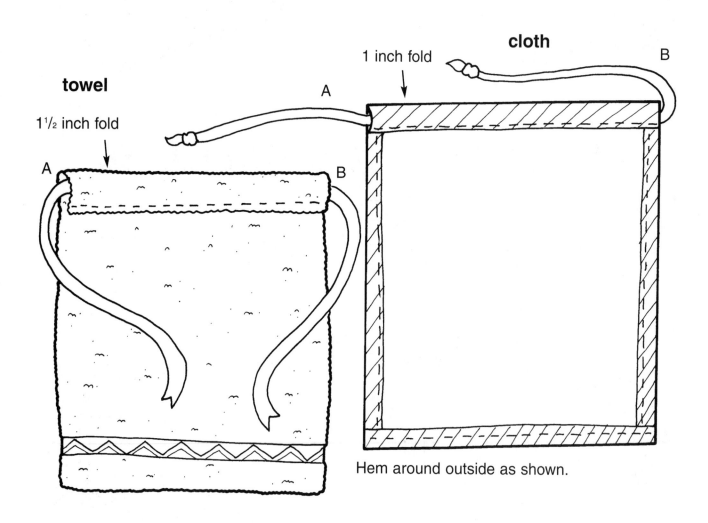

towel

1½ inch fold

A   B

cloth

1 inch fold

A   B

Hem around outside as shown.

Literature Selections,

Recipes, and

Activities

Pineapple Upside Down Cake

Alexander and the Terrible, Horrible, No Good, Very Bad Day
by Judith Viorst
(Macmillan Publishing Company, 1972)

Before You Cook

Alexander wakes up finding gum in his hair. He could tell immediately that it was going to be a "terrible, horrible, no good, very bad day." Alexander's troubles continue as the day progresses: his best friend at school is mean to him, he finds he has no dessert in his lunch bag, and his mother serves lima beans for dinner. He considers moving "down under" to Australia just to get away from all his problems.

If you've ever felt like your day has been turned "upside down," try forgetting your troubles by baking this delicious Pineapple Upside Down Cake.

From the Store

- sliced canned pineapple rings
- butter or margarine
- brown sugar
- eggs

From the Pantry

- solid vegetable shortening
- vanilla
- flour
- baking powder
- salt

Utensils to Gather

- measuring cups
- measuring spoons
- one 8" round cake pan
- two mixing bowls
- hand mixer
- rubber scraper
- one large plate
- colander or strainer
- hot plate

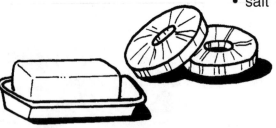

Pineapple Upside Down Cake Recipe

- 3 tablespoons margarine or butter
- 1 egg
- 20 oz. can pineapple rings
- 1 teaspoon vanilla
- ⅔ cup brown sugar
- 1 ¼ cups flour

- ⅓ cup shortening
- 1 ½ teaspoons baking powder
- ½ cup sugar
- ½ teaspoon salt

Preheat oven to 350 degrees. Melt margarine in cake pan using hot plate. Drain pineapple slices, saving ½ cup of drained syrup. Arrange pineapple slices in the bottom of the cake pan, placing them on top of the melted margarine. Place crumbled brown sugar on top of slices. In a bowl, cream together shortening and sugar. Add egg and vanilla and beat. In another bowl, mix together flour, baking powder, and salt. Add dry ingredients to creamed mixture, alternating with ½ cup of reserved pineapple syrup. Beat well. Spread this mixture over pineapple and smooth with scraper. Bake for 45-50 minutes. Remove from oven and let cake stand for five minutes. Invert on plate. Cut into wedges to serve.

Extra Helpings

1. Write and illustrate a story about a bad day you have had.
2. Change the story around to a "good day" story.
3. Find Australia on the map. Go to the library in your school or community. Check out a book about Australia and find out five interesting facts about that continent.

Books for Dessert

Balzola, Asun. *Munia and the Day Things Went Wrong.* Cambridge University Press, 1988.

Everitt, Betsy. *Mean Soup.* A Voyager Book, Harcourt Brace & Company, 1992.

Giff, Patricia Reilly. *Today Was a Terrible Day.* Viking, 1980.

Viorst, Judith. *I'll Fix Anthony.* Harper & Row Publishers, 1969.

Banana "Chips"

Anna Banana and Me
by Lenore Blegvad
(Simon & Schuster Children's Books, 1987)

Before You Cook

Anna Banana helps a young boy who is afraid of everything. He remembers to take Anna's advice when he is stranded alone. You can be fearless, too, when you try these banana "chips"!

From the Store

- bananas
- shredded coconut
- chopped walnuts
- chocolate syrup
- wheat germ

From the Pantry

- nothing

Utensils to Gather

- slicing knife
- four small bowls
- plates
- forks or toothpicks
- measuring cup
- waxed paper

Banana "Chips" Recipe

For each serving:
- 1 banana, peeled
- ½ cup shredded coconut
- ½ cup chocolate syrup
- ½ cup chopped nuts
- ½ cup wheat germ
- 1 piece of waxed paper

Slice banana onto waxed paper. Put coconut, chocolate syrup, nuts, and wheat germ in four separate bowls. Using a fork or toothpick, dip one banana slice in each of four bowls. Place on a plate, then enjoy!

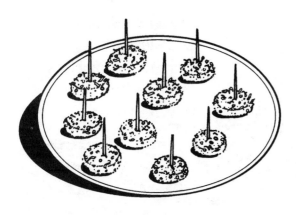

Extra Helpings

1. Besides monkeys, which animals like bananas? Make a list.
2. Tell someone about a time you were brave.
3. What are you afraid of? Tell someone older about your fear.
4. Name three or more ways to use bananas. Write them down.

Books for Dessert

Christelow, Eileen. *Five Little Monkeys Jumping on the Bed.* Clarion Books, 1989.

Cole, Joanna. *Anna Banana: 101 Jump-Rope Rhymes.* Scholastic, Inc., 1989.

Slobodkina, Esphyr. *Caps for Sale.* Harper Trophy, 1987.

Apple Slices and Dips

Apples and Pumpkins
by Anne Rockwell
(Scholastic Inc., 1991)

Before You Cook

This book will make you think about fall: leaves turning colors, apple and pumpkin picking, jack o'lanterns, trick-or-treating. Whether you pick your apples from the orchard or buy them at the grocery store, you'll find apple slices and dips fun to eat!

From the Store

- apples, any variety
- peanut butter, smooth or chunky
- caramel dip, found in produce section

From the Pantry

- cinnamon
- sugar

Utensils to Gather

- spoon
- plate
- two small bowls
- two spreading knives
- apple slicer or small, sharp knife

Apple Slices and Dips (cont.)

Apple Slices and Dips Recipe

- 4 apples
- ½ cup sugar
- 2 teaspoons cinnamon
- ¾ cup peanut butter, smooth or chunky style
- 18-20 oz. carton caramel dip

Mix sugar and cinnamon together in a small bowl. Measure peanut butter into another small bowl and open the caramel dip, arranging spreading knives next to these containers. Slice apples and arrange on plate. Dip each slice into one of three dips before eating.

Extra Helpings

1. Have an apple tasting party. Invite five or more friends. Taste several kinds of apples. Which one is your favorite? Take a vote and decide on the winning variety of apple.
2. Make a list of foods that are made from or contain apples.
3. Draw a picture of the life cycle of an apple tree.
4. Go apple picking. It's fun!

Books for Dessert

Kellogg, Steven. *Johnny Appleseed*. Morrow, 1988.

Maestro, Betsy. *How Do Apples Grow?* HarperCollins Publishers, 1992.

Micucci, Charles. *The Life and Times of the Apple*. Orchard Books, 1992.

Priceman, Marjorie. *How to Make Apple Pie and See the World*. Alfred A. Knopf, 1994.

Reasoner, Charles and Vicky Hardt. *Alphabite! A Funny Feast from A to Z*. Price Stern Sloan, 1989.

Pumpkin Raisin Nut Bread

The Biggest Pumpkin Ever
by Steven Kroll
(Scholastic Inc., 1984)

Before You Cook

Two mice take loving care of the same pumpkin, Clayton by day and Desmond by night. For a while, neither mouse knows about the other. The pumpkin grows enormous, the mice finally meet, and the pumpkin wins first prize in the town's pumpkin contest. This pumpkin is so big that even after carving it into a Jack o'lantern there is plenty left over to make pumpkin bread!

From the Store

- milk
- eggs
- butter
- canned pumpkin
- raisins
- nuts

From the Pantry

- flour
- baking powder
- baking soda
- salt
- ginger
- ground cloves
- solid vegetable shortening

Utensils to Gather

- one loaf pan
- two medium bowls
- one mixing spoon
- one scraper
- knife for slicing
- measuring cups and spoons
- hand mixer

Pumpkin Raisin Nut Bread (cont.)

Pumpkin Raisin Nut Bread Recipe

- 1 cup sugar
- ⅓ cup butter, softened
- ¼ cup milk
- 2 cups flour
- ½ teaspoon salt
- ½ teaspoon ginger
- ½ cup chopped nuts
- 2 eggs
- 1 cup canned pumpkin
- ¾ teaspoon cinnamon
- 2 teaspoons baking powder
- ¼ teaspoon baking soda
- ¼ teaspoon ground cloves
- 1 cup raisins

Preheat oven to 350 degrees. Using vegetable shortening, grease and then lightly flour the loaf pan; set aside. Cream together butter and sugar with the mixer. Add eggs and milk and beat well. Add pumpkin and blend. Mix together all of the dry ingredients, except nuts and raisins, in another bowl, then add to pumpkin mixture. Beat with mixer until well blended. Stir in the nuts and raisins. Pour into the prepared loaf pan and bake for 55-60 minutes. Cool and slice.

Extra Helpings

1. Carve a pumpkin into a jack o'lantern. Estimate how many seeds might be inside your pumpkin. Compare your estimate with the actual count. Were you close?
2. Measure the girth of your pumpkin with a piece of string. Then line up the string with a measuring tape. What is the circumference of your pumpkin in inches? In centimeters?
3. Roast the pumpkin seeds and eat them!

Books for Dessert

King, Elizabeth. *The Pumpkin Patch*. Dutton, 1990.

Miller, Edna. *Mousekin's Golden House*. Simon & Schuster Children's, 1971.

Titherington, Jeanne T. *Pumpkin, Pumpkin*. Greenwillow Books, 1986.

Blueberry Muffins

Blueberries for Sal
by Robert McCloskey
(Puffin Books, 1948)

Before You Cook

One summer day in Maine, a bear cub and a girl named Little Sal wander away from their blueberry-picking mothers. When Little Sal and the cub grow tired, they each sit down in the middle of a clump of blueberry bushes and eat until they are full. Realizing they are separated from their mothers, they go on a search, but each mistake the other's mother for their own! Eventually mothers and off-spring are reunited and go to their respective homes to store blueberries for the winter in their own unique way. You may not be able to store blueberries to save for winter, but you can make these delicious blueberry muffins.

From the Store

- eggs
- milk
- vegetable oil
- blueberries
- paper muffin liners

From the Pantry

- flour
- sugar
- baking powder
- salt
- cinnamon

Utensils to Gather

- measuring cups and spoons
- one small bowl
- one medium bowl
- one large spoon
- one rubber scraper
- two 6-muffin or one 12-muffin capacity tin

Blueberry Muffins (cont.)

Blueberry Muffins Recipe

- 1¾ cups flour
- ½ cup sugar
- 2½ teaspoons baking powder
- ½ teaspoon salt
- 1 teaspoon cinnamon
- ¾ cup milk
- ⅓ cup vegetable oil
- 1 egg
- ¾ – 1 cup blueberries, fresh or frozen

Preheat oven to 400 degrees. In medium bowl, stir together flour, sugar, baking powder, salt, and cinnamon. In small bowl, combine milk, oil, and egg. Add wet mixture to the dry ingredients, stirring until just moist. Add the blueberries and stir gently until evenly distributed. Spoon into lined muffin cups, filling each cup about ¾ full. Bake in oven for approximately 20 minutes or until muffin tops are lightly browned.

Extra Helpings

1. Get several different sized pails. Estimate how many blueberries each one would hold. How could you check your estimate?

2. Find out what bears like to eat besides blueberries.

3. Write your own story about a time when you got lost. Tell how you were reunited with your family.

4. Where is Maine? Find it on the United States map.

Books for Dessert

Betz, Dieter. *The Bear Family*. Morrow, 1992.

Degen, Bruce. *Jamberry*. HarperCollins Children's Books, 1995.

Hoban, Russell. *Bread and Jam for Frances*. Harper & Row, 1965.

King, Dave. *Amazing Bears*. Knopf, 1992.

Kuchall, Susan A. *Bears*. Troll Associates, 1982.

Numeroff, Laura Joffe. *If You Give a Moose a Muffin*. Harper Collins, 1991.

Slap with Hands Bread

Bread, Bread, Bread
by Ann Morris
(William Morrow & Co., Inc., 1993)

Before You Cook

People all over the world eat bread: fat bread, skinny bread, round bread, braided bread, bread with a hole in the middle. You can make a type of bread eaten in Mexico called a tortilla. It is not baked in an oven, does not come in a loaf, but does taste delicious! Try it, you'll like it!

From the Store

- optional: Jack cheese

From the Pantry

- flour
- baking powder
- salt
- shortening

Utensils to Gather

- measuring cups and spoons
- rolling pin
- medium bowl
- mixing spoon or scraper
- board to knead dough
- knife to cut dough
- skillet or frying pan
- hot plate

Slap with Hands Bread (cont.)

Slap with Hands Bread (Tortillas) Recipe

- 2 cups flour
- ½ teaspoon baking powder
- ½ teaspoon salt
- 3 tablespoons shortening
- ¾ cup warm water

In medium bowl, mix together flour, baking powder, and salt. Add shortening and use your fingers to cut it into the flour mixture until it is crumbly. Slowly add water until dough forms. Turn dough out onto lightly floured board and knead until smooth. Cut into 8 pieces and flatten each piece by slapping it on the palms of your hands or use a rolling pin. Fry tortillas in a hot greased skillet or frying pan. Optional: Sprinkle with grated Jack cheese and eat while still warm.

Extra Helpings

1. Try tasting different types of breads. Make a chart of how the breads are alike and different.

2. Take a trip to a bakery. Ask some questions about the different types of bread that are baked there.

3. Locate Mexico on a map. Is it north or south of the United States?

4. Look up information about Mexico. Make a replica of the Mexican flag. Write other things you learned about that country.

Books for Dessert

dePaola, Tomie. *Tony's Bread: An Italian Folktale*. Putnam, 1989.

Dooley, Norah. *Everybody Bakes Bread*. Carolrhoda Books, 1996.

Mitgutsch, Ali. *From Grain to Bread*. Carolrhoda Books, 1981.

Turner, Dorothy. *Bread*. Carolrhoda Books, 1989.

ABC Pretzels

Chicka Chicka Boom Boom
by Bill Martin, Jr. and John Archambault
(Scholastic Inc., 1989)

Before You Cook

In this charming alphabet book, all the letters climb up a coconut tree one by one. There are so many letters that they fall off the tree and become tangled, out of breath, stooped, and more. That night, after the moon comes out, the letters race to the top of the coconut tree to begin their activities all over again. You can have a good time with letters of the alphabet, too, when you make ABC pretzels.

From the Store

- dry yeast
- butter or margarine
- eggs
- coarse salt

From the Pantry

- flour
- plastic wrap
- sugar
- salt

Utensils to Gather

- large bowl
- small bowl
- rubber scraper
- wooden spoon
- wooden board for kneading dough
- knife
- pastry brush
- baking sheet

ABC Pretzels (cont.)

ABC Pretzels Recipe

- 2 cups warm water
- 2 packages dry yeast
- ½ cup sugar
- 2 teaspoons salt
- ¼ cup butter or margarine
- 1 egg
- 6-7½ cups flour
- 1 egg yolk
- 2 tablespoons water
- coarse salt

Preheat oven to 400 degrees. Pour warm water and yeast in large bowl. Stir until yeast dissolves. Add sugar, salt, margarine, 1 egg, and 3 cups flour. Beat with wooden spoon until smooth. Add enough flour to make a stiff dough. Scrape sides of bowl with rubber scraper. Cover dough tightly with plastic wrap. Refrigerate for 2 to 24 hours.

Turn dough out onto lightly floured board. Cut dough in half, then cut each half into 16 small, equal pieces. Roll each piece into a thin pencil shape about 20" long, then shape into a letter of the alphabet. Place on lightly greased baking sheet. Using small bowl and rubber scraper, blend together egg yolk and two tablespoons water. Brush ABC pretzels with this mixture using pastry brush. Sprinkle with coarse salt. Let rise in a warm place until double in bulk, about 25 minutes. Bake about 15 minutes or until pretzels are lightly brown. Remove from baking sheet to cool.

Note: Pretzels can be shaped according to the first letter of a child's name or into a child's favorite letter, etc.

Extra Helpings

1. Write your own poem. Can you give your words a beat or special rhythm?
2. Find out more about coconut trees. Where do they grow? Find the places on a map or globe.
3. What does a "full moon" mean? Find out more about the phases of the moon.

Books for Dessert

Banks, Kate. *Alphabet Soup*. Alfred A. Knopf, 1994.

Ehlert, Lois. *Eating the Alphabet from A to Z*. Harcourt Brace Jovanovich, 1993.

Elting, Mary and Michael Folsom. *Q is for Duck*. Clarion Books, 1980.

Hoban, Tana. *26 Letters and 96 Cents*. Greenwillow, 1987.

Tea Sandwich Shapes

A Cloak for the Dreamer
by Aileen Friedman
(Scholastic, Inc., 1995)

Before You Cook

A tailor asks each of his three sons to make a cloak for the archduke. Two sons are able to create beautiful cloaks by spending all of their time measuring, cutting, and sewing. But the youngest son, Misha, instead spends his time dreaming of traveling the world and looking at maps. The cloak Misha finally makes for the archduke is useless because it is made from circles of cloth patched together. Misha's brothers decide to tailor the useless cloak into a useful one as a going away present for their brother, Misha, the dreamer.

You may not be a tailor, but you can fashion these tea sandwiches into several interesting shapes.

From the Store

- cream cheese
- cucumber
- white bread, sliced
- parsley
- cherry tomatoes
- watercress
- herbal tea bags or canned fruit punch

From the Pantry

- nothing

Utensils to Gather

- knife for cutting
- knife for spreading
- plate
- glass or cup
- cookie cutters in a variety of shapes, if available

Tea Sandwich Shapes (cont.)

Tea Sandwich Shapes Recipe

- 8 slices white bread, crusts trimmed
- 8 oz. package cream cheese, either regular or reduced fat
- 1 small cucumber, cut into thin slices
- 1 small bunch parsley
- 1 small bunch watercress
- 1 basket cherry tomatoes

Make sandwiches using white bread, cream cheese, and cucumber slices. Cut sandwiches into shapes such as rectangle, circle, square, and triangle using cookie cutter shapes or a knife. Arrange on plate decorated with parsley, watercress, and cherry tomatoes. Serve with herbal tea or fruit punch.

Extra Helpings

1. What shapes can you think of? Draw them on a piece of paper.

2. Misha dreamed of seeing the world. Where do you dream of going? Find that special place on a globe or on a map of the world.

3. Misha's father was a very understanding man. Do you have an older friend or relative like him? Tell someone about it.

4. Make construction paper patterns. Choose one shape and cut it out of several different colors of paper in the same size, then arrange the pieces into a pattern that you like. Glue your pattern to another sheet of paper.

Books for Dessert

Birch, David. *The King's Chessboard*. Puffin Books, 1993.

Charles, N. N. *What Am I? Looking Through Shapes at Apples and Grapes*. Blue Sky Press—an imprint of Scholastic, Inc., 1994.

Hoban, Tana. *Circles, Triangles and Squares*. Macmillan, 1974.

McDermott, Gerald. *Arrow to the Sun: A Pueblo Indian Tale*. Puffin Books, 1991.

Tompert, Ann. *Grandfather Tang's Story*. Crown Publishers, Inc., 1990.

Uncle Donald's Umbrellas

The Cloud Book
by Tomie dePaola
(Scholastic, Inc., 1975)

Before You Cook

This is a nonfiction book describing different cloud formations. Knowing cloud formations can often help you predict the weather.

And if the clouds look like they will bring some rain, these "umbrellas" might be useful!

From the Store
- flour tortillas
- bread sticks
- butter

From the Pantry
- cinnamon-sugar mixture

Utensils to Gather
- knife for cutting
- knife for spreading
- plate

Uncle Donald's Umbrellas Recipe

For each serving:

- 1 tortilla
- 1 bread stick
- 1 tablespoon butter
- 1 tablespoon cinnamon-sugar mixture

Cut one tortilla in half. Use a knife to scallop the cut edge like an umbrella. Butter the tortilla halves and sprinkle with cinnamon/sugar mixture. Break the bread stick into two equal parts. Put the bread stick on a plate. Place the tortilla on top of the breadstick to make the snack look like an umbrella.

Extra Helpings

1. Go outside. See if you can find different shapes or animals in the cloud formations. Use your imagination!
2. Make a cloud picture. Use a piece of blue construction paper, cotton balls, and glue.
3. Look at the newspaper or listen to the television weather report. How many cloudy days does the weather report predict for the coming week? Keep your own record of the cloudy days for the week. Compare your record with the predictions.

Books for Dessert

Barrett, Judi. *Cloudy With a Chance of Meatballs*. Macmillan, 1978.

Goldsen, Louise. *Weather*. Scholastic, Inc., 1991.

Henley, Claire. *Stormy Days*. Hyperion Paperbacks for Children, 1993.

Sendak, Maurice. *Chicken Soup with Rice*. HarperCollins, 1962.

Suzuki, David and Barbara Hehner. *Looking at Weather*. Stoddart LB, 1991.

Zesty Pasta Salad

Daddy Makes the Best Spaghetti
by Anna Hines
(Clarion Books, 1986)

Before You Cook

Corey's daddy shares in tasks which keep the household running smoothly, including picking Corey up from day care, grocery shopping, and bathing Corey. Best of all, Daddy helps cook dinner, and he knows how to make the best spaghetti! If you like spaghetti or other pasta, try this zesty pasta salad.

From the Store

- macaroni or small shells
- celery
- tomato
- green onions
- green pepper
- zucchini
- cheese, Jack or cheddar
- Italian salad dressing

From the Pantry

- plastic wrap

Utensils to Gather

- one large bowl
- one mixing spoon
- cutting board
- knife for chopping
- hot plate
- large pot

Zesty Pasta Salad (cont.)

Zesty Pasta Salad Recipe

- ½ pound pasta
- ½ cup sliced green onions
- ½ cup chopped green pepper
- 1 cup cheese cubes
- ½ cup sliced celery
- ½ cup chopped zucchini
- 1 cup chopped tomatoes
- 6-8 oz. Italian dressing

Cook pasta according to package directions. Cool. Meanwhile, chop and slice vegetables, adjusting amounts according to taste. Place vegetables and cheese cubes in large bowl and toss. Add cooled pasta and toss again. Pour Italian dressing over all, toss again thoroughly, cover with plastic wrap, and chill until ready to eat.

Extra Helpings

1. What do your family members do at home to help each other?
2. Compare the weights of one cup of cooked and one cup of uncooked pasta. Also compare their volume. What did you discover?
3. Create a "pasta picture" by gluing various types of dry pasta onto construction paper.
4. Cover an empty frozen orange juice can with construction paper. Glue various types of dry pasta onto the can. When finished, wrap the can and give it to someone as a gift. It can be used as a pencil holder, or as a container for small kitchen utensils.

Books for Dessert

Coplans, Peta. *Spaghetti for Suzy*. Houghton Mifflin, 1993.

dePaola, Tomie. *Strega Nona*. Simon & Schuster Children's Books, 1979.

dePaola, Tomie. *Strega Nona's Magic Lessons*. Harcourt Brace Jovanovich, 1984.

Gelman, Rita G. *More Spaghetti, I Say*! Scholastic Inc., 1989.

Chocolate Chip Cookie Bars

The Doorbell Rang
by Pat Hutchins
(Scholastic Inc., 1986)

Before You Cook

Each time Mother tries to serve home-made chocolate chip cookies to Sam and Victoria, the doorbell rings. And each time friends and neighbors arrive, the children must recalculate the number of cookies each person receives so that everyone gets an equal number of cookies. Then Grandma enters with an enormous tray of cookies and saves the day! You can share these chocolate chip cookie bars with your friends and family and still have plenty of leftovers.

From the Store

- chocolate chips
- eggs
- butter
- chopped walnuts

From the Pantry

- flour
- brown sugar
- white sugar
- baking soda
- salt
- vanilla

Utensils to Gather

- one large mixing bowl
- one medium bowl
- one mixing spoon
- rubber scraper
- one 15" x 10" x 1" jelly roll pan

Chocolate Chip Cookie Bars (cont.)

Chocolate Chip Cookie Bars Recipe

- 2¼ cups flour
- 1 teaspoon baking soda
- 1 teaspoon salt
- 1 cup butter
- ¾ cup white sugar
- ¾ brown sugar
- 1 teaspoon vanilla
- 2 eggs
- 12 oz. chocolate chips
- 1 cup chopped walnuts

Preheat oven to 375 degrees. Combine flour, baking soda, and salt in medium bowl. Cream butter and sugars together with vanilla in large bowl. Beat eggs into creamed mixture. Gradually add dry ingredients to wet, mixing well. Stir in chocolate chips and nuts. Spread into greased jelly roll pan and bake for 20 to 25 minutes. Cool slightly and cut into 70 small squares.

Extra Helpings

1. Estimate how many chocolate chips are in a 12-oz. package. Count them. How close was your estimate?
2. What does the word "dozen" mean? What other foods or objects come in dozens? Make a list.
3. What if mother had baked 18 cookies? How could you share them equally with 2 friends, 3 friends, 6 friends, 9 friends?
4. Take a survey among your friends and family. Ask them what is their favorite cookie. What did you find out?

Books for Dessert

Aliki. *We Are Best Friends*. Greenwillow Books, 1982.

Carle, Eric. *Do You Want to be My Friend?* HarperCollins Children's Books, 1971.

deRegniers, Beatrice. *May I Bring a Friend?* Atheneum, 1964.

Falwell, Cathryn. *Feast for Ten.* Clarion, 1993.

Numeroff, Laura. *If You Give a Mouse a Cookie.* HarperCollins, 1985.

Fruits and Vegetables with Dips

Eating the Alphabet
by Lois Ehlert
(Harcourt Brace & Company, 1989)

Before You Cook

This book goes from "apple" to "zucchini," taking you through each letter by showing fruits and vegetables that begin with every letter of the alphabet. There is an excellent glossary which gives information about where each fruit and vegetable named in the book was first grown, plus other interesting information. You can enjoy some of your favorite fruits and vegetables when you try fruits and vegetables with dips.

From the Store

- celery
- broccoli
- carrots
- cauliflower
- green pepper
- cherry tomatoes
- banana
- orange

- apple
- strawberries
- milk
- instant vanilla pudding mix
- whipped topping
- chili sauce
- pickle relish
- whipped salad dressing

From the Pantry

- nothing

Utensils to Gather

- one small bowl
- one medium bowl
- two spoons
- two rubber scrapers
- one knife
- cutting board
- two plates or trays
- one hand mixer or rotary egg beater or whisk

Fruits and Vegetables with Dips (cont.)

Fruits and Vegetables with Dips Recipe

Vegetables:

- 1 basket cherry tomatoes
- 1 small bunch broccoli, cut into chunks
- 1 small head cauliflower, cut into chunks
- 1 cup whipped salad dressing
- ½ cup chili sauce (or to taste)
- 2 tablespoons pickle relish (or to taste)

Fruits:

- 2 each: bananas, oranges, apples
- 1 basket strawberries
- 1¾ cups milk
- 1 package vanilla instant pudding mix (4 serving size)
- 1 container whipped topping mix

Wash vegetables and cut into individual serving pieces (except cherry tomatoes, which may be left whole).

In small bowl, mix together portions of whipped salad dressing, chili sauce, and pickle relish to your taste (dip should be pink in color). Arrange vegetables on a plate or tray with dip in the center or next to the tray. Place spoon next to bowl of dip.

Wash fruit. Peel as needed and slice attractively. Hulls may be left on strawberries. In a medium bowl, blend together 1 ¾ cup cold milk with the package of instant vanilla pudding. Beat for about one minute. Add container whipped topping mix and whisk or beat again. Arrange fruit on plate or tray and serve with dip.

Extra Helpings

1. Make your own alphabet book. Cut out pictures from magazines that begin with each letter and paste on each page.

2. Find some unusual fruits and vegetables at the grocery store. Bring them to school to share with your teacher and classmates.

3. Survey your classmates and/or family. Find out what their favorite fruits are and what their favorite vegetables are. What did you find out?

4. Create breakfast, lunch, and dinner menus for one day. Include lots of fruits and vegetables.

Books for Dessert

Florian, Douglas. *Vegetable Garden*. Harcourt Brace Jovanovich, 1991.

Pallota, Jerry. *The Ocean Alphabet Book*. Charlesbridge, 1989.

Pallota, Jerry and Bob Thompson. *The Victory Garden Vegetable Alphabet Book*. Charlesbridge, 1992.

Westcott, Nadine. *The Giant Vegetable Garden*. Little, Brown & Co., 1981.

Refrigerator Pan Buns

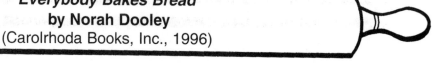

Everybody Bakes Bread
by Norah Dooley
(Carolrhoda Books, Inc., 1996)

Before You Cook

Carrie and Anthony are fighting on a rainy, boring Saturday morning while Mom is trying to make Italian bread. Mom sends Carrie on an errand to find a three-handled rolling pin. Carrie visits many neighbors and samples many different types of bread as she searches for this unusual rolling pin and discovers that many families are also baking bread on this rainy Saturday morning. Whether or not it is raining, you can keep your morning from becoming dull by making these Refrigerator Pan Buns.

From the Store

- butter or margarine
- dry yeast
- eggs

From the Pantry

- flour
- sugar
- salt

Utensils to Gather

- three 9" round cake pans
- one large mixing bowl
- one small bowl
- two spoons
- measuring cups
- measuring spoons
- mixing spoon
- board to knead dough
- plastic wrap

Refrigerator Pan Buns (cont.)

Refrigerator Pan Buns Recipe

- ¾ cup hot water
- ½ cup sugar
- 1 tablespoon salt
- 3 tablespoons butter or margarine
- 2½ cups flour and about 2¾ cups flour (about
  5 ¼ cups flour in all)
- 2 packages dry yeast
- 1 cup warm water
- 1 egg, beaten

Preheat oven to 375 degrees. In large bowl, mix together hot water, sugar, salt, and butter, stirring until butter melts. Set aside to cool. Meanwhile, dissolve yeast in 1 cup warm water. Wait until it is frothy, then add egg and 2½ cups flour. Beat until smooth. Add remaining flour and mix until a soft dough is formed. (You may not need all of the flour.) Turn dough out onto a lightly floured board and knead until smooth and elastic. Place in a greased bowl, turning dough around to grease both top and bottom. Cover dough with plastic wrap and store in refrigerator until ready to bake; dough may be stored for up to five days.

When ready to bake, punch dough down and turn out onto lightly floured board. Divide into three pieces. Make each piece into seven to nine buns by forming dough into balls. Place in three 9" greased round cake pans. Cover lightly and let rise in a warm place until doubled in size, about one hour. Bake for about 20 minutes or until lightly browned. Delicious!

Extra Helpings

1. Look through some old food magazines. Cut out pictures of breads or rolls to make a scrapbook.
2. Write a story about the different ways we use bread: to make a sandwich, to make stuffing, etc.
3. Why and how does yeast make bread rise? Find out and tell an adult.
4. What other types of flour can be used to make bread or rolls? Make a list.
5. What is your favorite "bread spread"? Ask your friends and family too. What did you find out?

Books for Dessert

Curtis, Neil and Peter Greenland. *How Bread Is Made*. Lerner Publishers, 1992.

Dooley, Norah. *Everybody Cooks Rice*. Scholastic Inc., 1991.

Morris, Ann. *Bread, Bread, Bread*. William Morrow & Co., Inc., 1993.

Heavenly Rice Pudding

Everybody Cooks Rice
by Norah Dooley
(Carolrhoda Books, 1991)

Before You Cook

Carrie's mom asks her to go outside and find her little brother, Anthony. As she searches, Carrie visits all of her neighbors. Each neighbor comes from a different country and each family is cooking rice using their own ethnic recipe. Carrie samples all the rice dishes as she follows the clues leading to her brother who has, of course, already returned home! Everybody cooks rice, so why not try this Heavenly Rice Pudding?

From the Store

- rice (not instant)
- vanilla pudding (not instant)
- milk

From the Pantry

- raisins

Utensils to Gather

- measuring cup for liquids
- one large bowl
- wire whisk
- spoon
- pots
- hot plate

Heavenly Rice Pudding (cont.)

Heavenly Rice Pudding Recipe

- 1 cup uncooked rice
- 2 cups water
- 1 package vanilla pudding mix, not instant
- 1 3/4 to 2 cups milk (see pudding directions for amount)
- 1/2 cup raisins

Cook rice as directed on package, using 1 cup of rice and 2 cups water. Cool. Prepare cooked pudding as directed on package, using mix and milk. Cool. Mix rice and pudding together in large bowl. Add 1/2 cup raisins. Serve in small paper cups or bowls.

Extra Helpings

1. Estimate how many grains of rice are in a pound. Count to check. (To make this task go more quickly, measure 1/4 lb. of rice. Count the grains, then multiply by four.)

2. The book describes how rice is cooked in Barbados, Puerto Rico, Vietnam, India, China, Haiti, and Northern Italy. Find each of those countries on a map or globe.

3. Write a story about how your family cooks rice. Ask your family to share a favorite rice recipe.

Books for Dessert

Brice, Raphaelle. *Rice: The Little Grain That Feeds the World*. Young Discovery Library, 1991.

Friedman, Ina. *How My Parents Learned to Eat*. Houghton Mifflin, 1987.

Merrison, Lynne. *Rice*. Carolrhoda Books, 1990.

Sendak, Maurice. *Chicken Soup With Rice*. Scholastic, Inc., 1992.

Tompert, Ann. *Bamboo Hats and a Rice Cake: a tale adapted from Japanese folklore*. Crown, 1993.

Cranberry Orange Sauce

The First Thanksgiving
by Jean George
(Philomel Books, 1993)

Before You Cook

This book describes how Squanto was kidnapped and sold to an Englishman, then finally returned to New England. The book also tells about the voyage of the Pilgrims as they sailed to the New World and created their home in Plymouth Harbor. Squanto and the Pilgrims met, signed a peace treaty, and began to learn from each other. Squanto taught the Pilgrims to find food in the forest as well as in the meadows and rivers. At the end of the book the author describes the first "Harvest Feast," the holiday we now call Thanksgiving.

The Pilgrims stuffed their wild turkeys with bread and cranberries. You can use cranberries, too, when you make Cranberry Orange Sauce.

From the Store

- cranberries
- frozen orange juice concentrate

From the Pantry

- sugar

Utensils to Gather

- one medium pot
- hot plate
- measuring cup
- spoon for stirring
- bowl or jar
- plastic wrap

Cranberry Orange Sauce (cont.)

Cranberry Orange Sauce Recipe

- 1 package cranberries
- 1 cup sugar
- 1½ cups orange juice from prepared concentrate (follow directions on can)

Wash and pick over cranberries, discarding any that are bruised or overripe. Place inspected berries in pot along with sugar and orange juice and stir. Bring mixture to a boil, then turn down heat and simmer until cranberries turn a deep red color and sauce thickens. Cool. Pour into bowl or jar and cover with plastic wrap. Store in refrigerator. This sauce tastes great with turkey or chicken!

Extra Helpings

1. Outline your hand on a piece of paper. Make your drawing into a turkey.
2. Find out where cranberries grow and how they ripen.
3. Write down all the things you are thankful for.
4. Estimate how many cranberries are in the bag. Count them. How close was your estimate to the actual count?

Books for Dessert

Dalgliesh, Alice. *The Thanksgiving Story*. Macmillan, 1988.

Gorsline, Marie and Douglas. *North American Indians*. Random House, 1978.

Kroll, Steven. *Oh, What a Thanksgiving*. Scholastic Inc., 1988.

Raphael, Elaine and Don Bolognese. *The Story of the First Thanksgiving*. Scholastic Inc., 1991.

Waters, Kate. *Samuel Eaton's Day*. Scholastic Inc., 1993.

Monkey Bread

Five Little Monkeys Jumping on the Bed
by Eileen Christelow
(Clarion Books, 1989)

Before You Cook

As in the traditional nursery rhyme, five monkeys jump on a bed instead of getting ready for sleep. Finally Mama is able to get them to bed so that she, too, can go to bed. Try this recipe for "Monkey Bread." It's so delicious you'll want to jump up and down when you taste it!

From the Store

- refrigerated buttermilk biscuits
- butter or margarine

From the Pantry

- sugar
- cinnamon

Utensils to Gather

- two 9" x 5" x 2½" bread pans
- knife
- paper bag
- small pot
- spoon for stirring
- hot plate

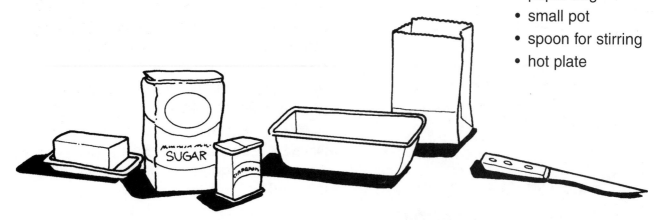

Monkey Bread (cont.)

Monkey Bread Recipe

- 4 tubes refrigerated buttermilk biscuits
- ¾ cup sugar
- 1 teaspoon cinnamon
- 1 cup sugar
- ¾ cup butter (1½ sticks)
- ¾ teaspoon cinnamon

Preheat oven to 350 degrees. Pour ¾ cup sugar and 1 teaspoon cinnamon in a paper bag and shake to mix. Open each tube of biscuits and cut each biscuit into four parts. Shake pieces in bag with sugar/cinnamon mixture. Place coated pieces evenly in the two greased bread pans. Put 1 cup sugar, ¾ cup butter or margarine, and ¾ teaspoon cinnamon in small pot and bring to a boil, stirring constantly. Boil for 1 minute. Pour half of mixture evenly over each pan of biscuits. Bake for ½ hour.

Extra Helpings

1. Why is it so much fun to jump on a bed? Write a story.
2. How do you get ready for bed? Describe your bedtime routine to a friend.
3. Find five facts about monkeys. Write them down.
4. Look at a world map. Where do monkeys live?

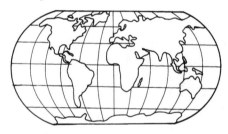

Books for Dessert

Ahlberg, Allan. *Ten in a Bed.* Viking, 1989.

Aylesworth, James. *One Crow: A Counting Rhyme.* HarperCollins Children's Books, 1990.

Brown, Marc, ed. *Hand Rhymes.* Dutton Children's Books, 1985.

Hammond, Franklin. *Ten Little Ducks.* Scholastic Inc., 1993.

Reys, Margaret & H. A. *Curious George.* Scholastic Inc., 1973

Strawberry "Shake One in the Hay"

Frank and Ernest
by Alexandra Day
(Scholastic, Inc., 1991)

Before You Cook

Frank and Ernest run Mrs. Miller's diner for three days. They have to learn a new vocabulary in order to make the diner run smoothly, such as finding out the meaning of "shake one in the hay." You'll soon know what it means, too, when you try the recipe on the following page.

From the Store

- vanilla or strawberry ice cream
- fresh or frozen strawberries
- milk

From the Pantry

- sugar

Utensils to Gather

- blender
- one scraper
- two large glasses
- measuring cups
- measuring spoons

Strawberry "Shake One in the Hay" (cont.)

Strawberry "Shake one in the Hay" Recipe

- 8 oz. milk
- 6-8 large strawberries or ½ cup frozen strawberries, defrosted
- ½ pint vanilla or strawberry ice cream
- 1 tablespoon sugar, if desired

Pour 8 oz. or 1 cup of milk into blender. Add the vanilla or strawberry ice cream to the fresh or defrosted frozen strawberries. Blend. Taste and add sugar, if desired. Pour and scrape into two large glasses.

Extra Helpings

1. Make up some new names for foods you like. Write them down.
2. How would you have run Mrs. Miller's diner? Write your story.
3. Look at the front and end pages of the book. Can you tell why the foods are given these "special" names? Talk it over with your parent(s).
4. Have you ever been to a diner? What makes it different from a regular restaurant? In what ways are they the same?
5. Create a new menu for an imaginary diner of your own. What would you serve for breakfast, lunch, and dinner?

Books for Dessert

Day, Alexandra. *Carl's Afternoon in the Park*. Farrar, Strauss & Giroux, Inc., 1991.

Day, Alexandra. *Frank and Ernest on the Road*. Scholastic, Inc., 1994.

Day, Alexandra. *Frank and Ernest Play Ball*. Scholastic, Inc., 1994.

Gibbons, Gail. *Marge's Diner*. Thomas Y. Crowell Jr. Books, 1989.

Lester, Helen. *Me First*. Houghton Mifflin Company, 1992.

Chocolate Marshmallow Pie

Gator Pie
by Louise Mathews
(Sundance Publishing, 1995)

Before You Cook

Alice and Alvin find a pie and agree to divide it in half. But soon another alligator arrives and demands a share. Alice and Alvin agree to divide the pie into thirds. More alligators arrive and demand a piece of the pie, until the pie will need to be divided into 100 pieces. If that isn't enough, a fight breaks out over whether the pieces will be equal. While the other alligators are fighting, Alice and Alvin race off into the swamp and divide the pie in two, just as they began. You can share this delicious chocolate marshmallow pie with your friends. Try not to share it with too many friends, because the pieces of this treat will be too small!

From the Store

- milk
- large marshmallows
- semi-sweet chocolate squares
- whipped topping
- prepared graham cracker crust

From the Pantry

- nothing

Utensils to Gather

- pot
- spoon
- scraper
- pie server

Chocolate Marshmallow Pie (cont.)

Chocolate Marshmallow Pie Recipe

- 30 large marshmallows
- 2 oz. square semi-sweet chocolate
- ½ cup milk
- 8 oz. container whipped topping
- 1 prepared graham cracker crust

Melt chocolate in medium pot. Add marshmallows and milk. Stir until marshmallows melt. Cool slightly. Fold in whipped topping. Pour into graham cracker crust and refrigerate before serving, about 2-3 hours.

Extra Helpings

1. Find out some interesting facts about chocolate and share them with your family.
2. What are your favorite foods containing chocolate? Make a list.
3. What do you know about alligators? Find three interesting facts and tell an adult.
4. What is a swamp? Where can you find one?
5. Do you like to share? Tell your family about it.
6. Invite some friends to share the pie!

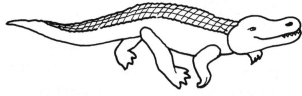

Books for Dessert

Leedy, Loreen. *Fraction Action*. Holiday House, Inc., 1994.

McMillan, Bruce. *Eating Fractions*. Scholastic, Inc., 1992.

Moncure, Jane B. *How Many Ways Can You Cut a Pie?* Child's World, Inc., 1987.

Silverstein, Shel. *Giraffe and a Half*. HarperCollins Children's Books, 1964.

Hero Sandwich

The Giant Jam Sandwich
by John Vernon Lord
(Houghton Mifflin, 1987)

Before You Cook

The people of the town of Itching Down have a problem—pesky wasps humming and buzzing and swarming around their food. The townspeople hold a meeting and come up with a unique idea—build a giant jam sandwich to trap the wasps. Will the wasps go for the bait? Read the story to find out! You can make a giant sandwich, too, when you follow this recipe for Hero Sandwich.

From the Store

- French bread
- mayonnaise
- lettuce
- tomatoes
- sliced turkey
- sliced roast beef
- sliced American cheese
- sliced Swiss cheese
- sliced pickles
- sliced ripe olives
- medium red onion
- sprouts
- Italian salad dressing

From the Pantry

- nothing

Utensils to Gather

- knife for cutting
- knife for spreading
- large bread board or other surface for assembling sandwich
- plates
- paper towels
- can opener

Hero Sandwich (cont.)

Hero Sandwich Recipe

- 1 loaf French bread cut in half lengthwise
- 1 jar mayonnaise, 16 oz.
- lettuce leaves, washed and dried with paper towels
- 2-3 sliced tomatoes
- ½ pound sliced turkey
- ½ pound sliced roast beef
- ½ pound sliced American cheese
- ½ pound sliced Swiss cheese
- pickle and olive slices
- thinly sliced red onion rings
- 40 oz. package of sprouts
- 1 bottle Italian salad dressing

Cut bread loaf in half lengthwise. Spread halves with mayonnaise. On one half place lettuce leaves, sliced tomatoes, meats, and cheeses. Sprinkle with pickle and olive slices, sprouts, and thinly sliced red onion rings. Drizzle with Italian dressing. Place other half of French bread on top of sandwich and slice. Optional: Serve with carrot and/or celery sticks and your favorite chips.

Extra Helpings

1. Choose any item—chocolate bar, watermelon, pickle, etc.—and imagine it becoming gigantic. Write a story about it.

2. What is your favorite lunch menu? Write it down and share it with your family.

3. The man in this story had a giant pie next. If you were going to have pie for desert, what kind would you like to have? Tell someone.

4. How many people do you estimate could eat the man's jam sandwich? Make guesses with your friends.

5. At the beginning of the book the children were having a picnic. Draw a picture of a picnic you've had.

Books for Dessert

Holland, Marion. *A Big Ball of String*. Random Books for Young Readers, 1993.

Kroll, Steven. *The Biggest Pumpkin Ever*. Scholastic, Inc., 1984.

Spurr, Elizabeth. *The Biggest Birthday Cake in the World*. Harcourt Brace, 1991.

Willard, Nancy. *The High Rise Glorious Skittle Skat Roarious Sky Pie Angel Food Cake*. Harcourt Brace, 1990.

Dressed-Up Porridge

Goldilocks and the Three Bears
by Jan Brett
(Putnam Publishing Group, 1990)

Before You Cook

When Goldilocks discovers the three bears' cottage in the woods, she decides to enter. She eats their porridge, breaks a chair, and falls asleep upstairs. The three bears are surprised when they get home and discover their guest sleeping in Baby Bear's bed! Goldilocks ate porridge and so can you when you try this recipe!

From the Store

- packet of instant oatmeal
- raisins
- sliced almonds
- milk

From the Pantry

- cinnamon
- brown sugar

Utensils to Gather

- saucepan
- mixing spoon
- measuring cup
- bowls
- spoons
- hot plate

Dressed-Up Porridge (cont.)

Dressed-Up Porridge Recipe

- 1 packet instant oatmeal
- ½ cup boiling water
- ¼ cup raisins
- ½ teaspoon cinnamon
- 1 tablespoon sliced almonds
- 1 tablespoon brown sugar (more or less to taste)
- milk to pour on cereal

Prepare instant oatmeal according to package directions. Stir in raisins, cinnamon, and sliced almonds. Spoon into a bowl and serve with brown sugar and milk.

Extra Helpings

1. Act out the story of Goldilocks. Ask some of your friends to help. Invite other friends to see the show.
2. Go to the library. Find some interesting facts about bears. Write a report.
3. Pretend that you are Goldilocks. Write a letter to the three bears apologizing for what you did to their food and furniture.
4. Goldilocks entered the three bears' cottage without permission. What do you think of that? Talk it over with an adult.

Books for Dessert

Brett, Jan. *Goldilocks and the Three Bears*. Putnam Publishing Group, 1990.

Galdone, Paul. *The Magic Porridge Pot*. Houghton Mifflin, 1979.

Marshall, James. *Goldilocks and the Three Bears*. Dial Books For Young Readers, 1988.

Milne, A. A. *Winnie the Pooh*. Dutton Children's Books, 1992.

Stevens, Janet retold by. *Goldilocks and the Three Bears*. Holiday House, 1986.

Bird Nests

Grandfather Tang's Story
by Ann Tompert
(Crown Publishers, 1990)

Before You Cook

Using tangrams to illustrate his story, Grandfather Tang tells Little Soo a dramatic tale about a friendship between two fairies, Wu Ling and Chou. Wu Ling and Chou are able to transform themselves into different animals, but when they turn into geese, tragedy strikes. The fairies then learn an important lesson about loyalty between friends. Many birds, including geese, make nests for their homes. You can make a "bird nest," too, using chow mein noodles.

From the Store

- jelly beans
- butterscotch chips
- chow mein noodles

From the Pantry

- smooth peanut butter
- waxed paper
- chocolate chips

Utensils to Gather

- measuring cup and spoons
- medium pot
- hot plate
- spoon

Bird Nests (cont.)

Bird Nests Recipe

- ½ cup peanut butter
- 12 oz. chocolate chips
- 12 oz. butterscotch chips
- 12 oz. chow mein noodles
- 16 oz. or 1 pound jelly bean candies

Melt ½ cup peanut butter with packages of chocolate and butterscotch bits in pan over low heat, stirring constantly. Add noodles and mix to coat them. Drop covered noodles by spoonfuls onto waxed paper. Shape into "bird nests," using your thumb to make an indentation in the center. Put jelly beans in center to represent "eggs." Place in refrigerator to harden.

Extra Helpings

1. Make your own set of tangrams using the pattern which appears in the back of Grandfather Tang's Story. Use the tangrams to create your own animals.
2. Visit the library to find another Chinese folktale.
3. Write a story about friendship. Share it with one of your friends.
4. Find China on a map of the world.

Books for Dessert

Charles, N.N. *What Am I? Looking at Shapes through Apples and Grapes.* Blue Sky Press, 1994.

Chermayeff, Ivan and Jane. *First Shapes.* Abrams, 1991.

Cohen, Miriam. *Best Friends.* Macmillan Publishing Co., Inc., 1971.

Ehlert, Lois. *Color Farm.* Lippincott, 1990.

Sharmat, Marjorie. *The 329th Friend.* Macmillan Publishing Co., Inc., 1992.

Wildsmith, Brian. *Animal Shapes.* Oxford University Press, 1980.

Yen, Clara. *Why Rat Comes First: A Story of the Chinese Zodiac.* Children's Book Press, 1991.

Dirt Cake

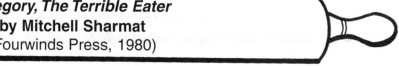

Gregory, The Terrible Eater
by Mitchell Sharmat
(Fourwinds Press, 1980)

Before You Cook

Gregory, the goat, is considered to be a terrible eater by his parents. He prefers to eat fruits, vegetables, eggs, fish, bread and butter—not the boxes, rugs, bottle caps, old shoes, and shirts preferred by his parents. After a doctor suggests introducing new foods to Gregory one at a time, Gregory has a binge on flat tires, a broken violin, and half a car—much to the delight of his parents! Hopefully, your eating habits will revert back to normal after you try this recipe for Dirt Cake.

From the Store
- cream-filled chocolate cookies
- powdered sugar
- cream cheese
- whipped topping
- instant vanilla pudding
- butter
- milk

From the Pantry
- nothing

Utensils to Gather
- rolling pin
- one small bowl
- one large bowl
- one 9"x12" inch baking pan or one large glass bowl
- wire whisk
- rubber scraper
- spoon
- plastic food storage bag

Dirt Cake (cont.)

Dirt Cake Recipe

- 20 oz. package chocolate sandwich cookies
- ³/₄ stick softened butter
- 1 cup powdered sugar
- 8 oz. softened cream cheese
- 3 cups milk
- 2 packages instant vanilla pudding mix
- 12 oz. container whipped topping

Crush cookies using rolling pin and plastic bag. Set aside. In small bowl, whisk together butter, cream cheese, and sugar. Set aside. In large bowl, mix pudding and milk according to package directions. Add whipped topping and butter, cream cheese and sugar mixture.

Layer ingredients in baking pan or glass bowl as follows:

- ¹/₃ cookies
- ¹/₂ pudding mixture
- ¹/₃ cookies
- ¹/₂ pudding mixture

Finish with cookies on top of cake. Add plastic flowers on top, if desired. Also, gummy worms can be added to the cake itself. Dig in and enjoy!

Extra Helpings

1. Do goats really eat old shoes, tin cans, violins and cars? Find the facts, then share them with your family.

2. After you find out what goats eat, make up a menu for one day. What would Gregory like to eat for breakfast, lunch, and dinner? Find pictures in magazines, cut them out, and paste them onto Gregory's menu or paper "place mats."

3. Gregory's parents enjoyed eating trash. Find a piece of trash in your classroom. Think about how you could recycle it rather than throwing it out. Write down your idea and draw a picture.

Books for Dessert

Brown, Marc. *D. W. the Picky Eater*. Little, Brown and Company, 1995.

Ehlert, Lois. *Eating the Alphabet: Fruits and Vegetables from A to Z*. Harcourt Brace Jovanovich, 1994.

Wescott, Nadine. *The Giant Vegetable Garden*. Little, Brown and Company, 1981.

Ladybug Salad

The Grouchy Ladybug
by Eric Carle
(HarperCollins, 1986)

Before You Cook

The grouchy ladybug is looking for a fight with anyone, no matter what his or her size. But when she finally meets her match, she winds up where she belongs—at home, eating aphids. Try making this edible ladybug salad. You'll have fun!

Note: in order to get 8 or more pieces of curly tomato pasta, you may need to purchase tri-color pasta and separate the red pieces for cooking.

From the Store
- red gelatin
- leaf lettuce
- curly tomato pasta

From the Pantry
- chocolate chips
- raisins

Utensils to Gather
- medium bowl
- mixing spoon
- measuring cup
- custard cups
- hot plate

Ladybug Salad (cont.)

Ladybug Salad Recipe

- 1 large leaf of lettuce for each salad
- 6 oz. package red gelatin
- boiling water
- red or tomato curly pasta, 8 pieces per salad
- ⅓ cup chocolate chips
- ¼ cup raisins

Wash lettuce and set aside. Prepare red gelatin according to package directions. Prepare needed amount of curly tomato pasta according to package directions. Pour gelatin into individual custard cups. Place in refrigerator to jell. When jelled, turn out onto leaf lettuce-lined plate. Make sure the rounded side of the gelatin is facing up. Decorate with chocolate chips for "spots," raisins for "eyes" and curly pasta for "legs" and "antennae."

Extra Helpings

1. Write down your schedule for one day.

Example: 6:30 A.M.   Get up
            7:00 A.M.   Eat breakfast
            8:00 A.M.   School begins

2. Figure out what time it is in different parts of the world. Choose six cities. Find them on a world map and then find out the correct time. Example: if it's 7:00 A.M. in Chicago, it's 8:00 A.M. in New York City.
3. Make a clock out of a large paper plate. Use small pieces of tagboard for the hands and a paper fastener to attach the hands to the plate.
4. Think about different words we use to describe the passage of time. Make a list. Some examples are: almost, past, after, etc.
5. Look for different types of clocks in your house and at your friends' and relatives' homes. Draw a picture of each one and make into a booklet. Examples: analog, digital, grandfather, etc.

Books for Dessert

Burns, Marilyn. *This Book is About Time.* Little, Brown & Co., 1978.

Dijs, Carla. *What Do I Do at Eight O'clock?* Simon and Schuster, 1993.

McMillan, Bruce. *Time to—.* Lothrop, 1989.

Singer, Marilyn. *Nine O'clock Lullaby.* HarperCollins Publishers, 1991.

Wallace-Brodeur, Ruth. *Home by Five.* Macmillan, 1992.

Yummy Vegetable Soup

Growing Vegetable Soup
by Lois Ehlert
(Scholastic Inc., 1987)

Before You Cook

A father and child plant various types of seeds and sprouts, care for the plants, and wait for them to grow. At last they harvest their garden and bring the vegetables home. They then prepare a pot of delicious vegetable soup.

Making vegetable soup is easy when you follow the simple directions on the following page.

From the Store

- onion
- potato
- carrots
- celery
- green beans
- zucchini
- tomatoes
- frozen peas
- chicken or vegetable stock cubes
- parsley
- crackers

From the Pantry

- salt
- pepper
- thyme

Utensils to Gather

- one large soup pot
- ladle
- knife
- cutting board
- can opener
- hot plate

Yummy Vegetable Soup (cont.)

Yummy Vegetable Soup Recipe

- 1-2 onions
- 2-3 stalks celery
- 4 carrots
- 3 potatoes
- ½ pound green beans or a 10 oz. package frozen green beans
- 28 oz. can whole peeled tomatoes, with juice
- ¼ to ½ pound peas or a 10 oz. package frozen peas
- 1 zucchini
- 1 small bunch parsley
- 8 cups water
- 8 stock cubes
- 1 tablespoon salt, or to taste
- ½ teaspoon pepper, or to taste
- 1 teaspoon thyme, or to taste
- 1 box crackers

Wash and peel vegetables as needed and slice. Place in large soup pot along with stock cubes and water. Add salt, pepper, and thyme to taste. Bring to a boil, reduce heat, and simmer until vegetables are done. Adjust seasonings. Serve piping hot with crackers.

Extra Helpings

1. Buy some small peat pots and seeds. Plant an indoor garden. When your plants get big, transplant them outdoors.
2. Make a list of your favorite vegetables.
3. Try a new vegetable that you haven't tasted before.
4. Rabbits like to eat vegetables. Get a few friends together and do the Bunny Hop dance together for exercise!
5. Draw a picture of a garden plot. Show where you would place each row of plants and label them.

Books for Dessert

Ehlert, Lois. *Eating the Alphabet*. Harcourt Brace Jovanovich, 1993.

Ehlert, Lois. *Planting a Rainbow*. Harcourt Brace & Co., 1992.

Rattigan, Jama Kim. *Dumpling Soup*. Little, Brown & Company, 1993.

Westcott, Nadine. *The Giant Vegetable Garden*. Little Brown & Company, 1981.

Monster Carrot Creature

The Hungry Thing
by Jan Slepian and Ann Seidler
(Scholastic, Inc., 1988)

Before You Cook

The Hungry Thing comes to town and demands food, but the townspeople can't understand what the Hungry Thing wants because it uses words like "shmancakes," "tickles," "hookies," and "gollipops." It takes a clever boy to figure out the lingo of the Hungry Thing. You will be a "hungry thing" no longer after you make this "monstrous" snack.

From the Store
- slivered almonds
- carrots

From the Pantry
- raisins
- peanut butter

Utensils to Gather
- knife
- vegetable peeler
- spoon
- measuring spoon

Monster Carrot Creature Recipe

- 1 carrot
- 2 raisins
- 1 tablespoon peanut butter
- about 4 pieces of slivered almonds

Wash and peel carrot. Cut a v-shape at the large end to make a "mouth." Using peanut butter as "glue," place two raisins above the mouth as "eyes" and almonds inside the mouth as "teeth."

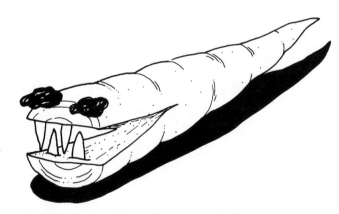

Extra Helpings

1. Make up a guessing game using silly or rhyming words for clues like "papples" for apples or "shmarrots" for carrots. Create and display the list.

2. Create another "Hungry Thing" using paper and crayons and a paper bag. Put it on your hand when you're finished and use it as a puppet.

3. Why do you think the townspeople couldn't understand what the "Hungry Thing" wanted to eat? Tell your family.

Books for Dessert

Baumann, Kurt. *The Hungry One*. North-South Books, 1993.

Calhoun, Mary. *The Hungry Leprechaun*. Morrow Jr. Books, 1962.

Demarest, Chris L. *No Peas for Nellie*. Simon & Schuster Children's Books, 1991.

Ga'g, Wanda. *Funny Thing*. Putnam Publishing Group/Sandcastle Books, 1991.

Leedy, Loreen. *The Monster Money Book*. Holiday House, 1992.

Slepian, Jan and Ann Seidler. *The Hungry Thing Returns*. Scholastic, 1990.

Orange Muffins

If You Give a Moose a Muffin
by Laura Joffe Numeroff
(Scholastic Inc., 1992)

Before You Cook

If you give a moose a muffin, he'll ask for more and more things: jam, some old socks, materials to make a puppet show, and, eventually, more muffins!

Reading this hilarious story will make you want some muffins too, so give these fragrant orange muffins a try.

From the Store
- orange
- orange juice
- butter
- eggs

From the Pantry
- flour
- sugar
- baking powder
- baking soda
- salt
- raisins
- paper muffin liners

Utensils to Gather
- measuring cups and spoons
- muffin tins
- medium bowl
- food processor or grater
- sharp knife and cutting board
- scraper
- hand mixer
- mixing spoon

Orange Muffins (cont.)

Orange Muffins Recipe

- 1 whole orange
- ½ cup orange juice
- ¾ cup sugar
- 1 teaspoon baking soda
- ¼ teaspoon salt
- 1 egg
- ½ cup butter at room temperature
- 1½ cups flour
- 1 teaspoon baking powder
- ½ cup raisins

Either cut orange into small pieces and run in food processor with ½ cup orange juice until finely chopped, or grate orange rind and cut orange into very small pieces. Add egg and butter to processed or finely chopped orange and mix well. Beat in sugar. Mix together all dry ingredients and add to the wet mixture. Blend well. Stir in raisins. Bake at 350 degrees for 15 minutes or until lightly browned. Serve warm with butter.

Extra Helpings

1. Go to the library and find some interesting facts about the moose. Write down your five favorite facts.
2. What is your favorite kind of muffin? Ask your friends and relatives, too. What did you find out?
3. Make an animal puppet out of an old, clean sock. Ask a parent or relative to help.
4. Write a funny story about another animal who comes to your house. What will it ask for?

Books for Dessert

Carlstrom, Nancy White. *Moose in the Garden.* Harper & Row Publishers, 1990.

Giganti, Paul, Jr. *Each Orange Had Eight Slices.* Greenwillow, 1992.

Numeroff, Laura. *If You Give a Mouse a Cookie.* Harper & Row, 1991.

Proysen, Alf. *Mrs. Pepperpot and the Moose.* R & S Books, 1991.

Bread Dough "Inchworms"

Inch by Inch
by Leo Lionni
(Astor-Honor, 1960)

Before You Cook

An inchworm measures the parts of various birds: the tail of a robin, the neck of a flamingo, the beak of a toucan, etc. But when he is asked to measure the immeasurable song of a nightingale, he slowly "inches" out of sight! You can create an "inchworm" that disappears as you eat it by using packaged bread dough.

From the Store

- frozen bread dough
- butter
- green food coloring

From the Pantry

- flour
- raisins

Utensils to Gather

- knife
- cutting board
- cookie sheet
- pastry brush
- small pot
- one small custard cup
- hot plate

Bread Dough "Inchworms" (cont.)

Bread Dough "Inchworms" Recipe

- ¼ cup butter
- 1 loaf frozen bread dough, defrosted
- 1 bottle green food coloring
- ¼ cup raisins

Melt butter in small pot, cool slightly, then pour into a small custard cup. Mix in green food coloring and set aside. Divide defrosted bread dough into 6-8 small pieces. Dip each piece in flour and roll into an "inchworm" with your hands. Place on cookie sheet and add 2 raisins for eyes. With pastry brush, paint each shape with green butter. Bake at 350 degrees for about 15 minutes.

Extra Helpings

1. Go to the library to find interesting facts about inchworms. Write what you find out.
2. Use frozen bread dough to make your initials. Bake them, too.
3. What makes bread rise? Find out.
4. Various birds are mentioned in this book. Can you find six other types of birds and name them?
5. Draw a picture of your favorite bird in its habitat.

Books for Dessert

Allen, Pam. *Who Sank the Boat?* Putnam, 1989.

Ginsburg, Mirra. *Mushroom in the Rain*. Macmillan Children's Group, 1990.

Morimoto, Junko. *The Inch Boy and Fables*. Puffin Books, 1988.

Myller, Rolf. *How Big is a Foot?* Dell, 1991.

Bedtime Snacks

Ira Sleeps Over
by Bernard Waber
(Houghton Mifflin, 1972)

Before You Cook

Ira is going to his first sleepover at his friend Reggie's house and can't decide whether to take his teddy bear, Tah Tah. His mother tells Ira to bring Tah Tah along, but his sister tells him to keep Tah Tah home because Reggie might laugh at him. What should Ira do? Read this story to find out what Ira decides! Meanwhile, if you need a bedtime snack, try hot cocoa and cinnamon toast.

From the Store

- cocoa mix packets
- marshmallows
- sliced white bread
- butter

From the Pantry

- sugar
- cinnamon

Utensils to Gather

- toaster or toaster oven
- tea kettle
- cups or mugs
- spoons
- small bowl

Bedtime Snacks Recipe

- 2 cups boiling water
- 2 packets cocoa mix
- 2 pieces bread
- marshmallows
- 2 tablespoons butter
- 2 tablespoons cinnamon/sugar mixture

Use packet directions to make hot cocoa and float marshmallows in each mug. Meanwhile, toast 2 slices of bread. Spread each slice with 1 tablespoon of butter. Sprinkle with cinnamon/sugar mixture. Cut toast into triangles and eat with a mug or cup of cocoa. Sweet dreams!

Extra Helpings

1. Do you have a teddy bear or other stuffed animal that you sleep with? Tell a friend about it.

2. Have you ever gone to a sleep over at a friend or relative's house? Draw a picture to illustrate the event.

3. Make up a scary ghost story and tell it to a friend.

4. What are the things you like to do with, or for, a friend? Make a list.

Books for Dessert

Baylor, Byrd. *Amigo*. Simon & Schuster Children's Books, 1989.

Bunnett, Rochelle. *Friends in the Park*. Checkerboard Press, Inc., 1993.

Clements, Andrew. *Big Al*. Simon & Schuster Children's Books, 1991.

Heine, Helme. *Friends*. Macmillan, 1982.

Lobel, Arnold. *Frog and Toad are Friends*. HarperCollins, 1970.

Scrambled Eggs

It Wasn't My Fault
by Helen Lester
(Houghton Mifflin Company, 1985)

Before You Cook

Murdley Gurdson has many accidents, usually his own fault.
As he goes for a walk one day, a bird lays an egg on his head. The bird tries to blame another creature, who blames another creature, and so on, until an entire parade of squabbling animals forms. At the end of the story, the animals return to Murdley's house, where they make scrambled eggs.

Make your own scrambled eggs by following this recipe.

From the Store

- eggs
- butter
- milk
- bread, optional

From the Pantry

- salt
- pepper

Utensils to Gather

- frying pan or skillet
- egg turner or metal spatula
- medium bowl
- wire whisk
- measuring spoons
- hot plate
- toaster, optional

82

Scrambled Eggs (cont.)

Scrambled Eggs Recipe

- 6 eggs
- 2-3 tablespoons butter
- ½ teaspoon salt
- ⅛ teaspoon pepper
- milk
- bread for toast, optional

Crack the eggs into a bowl. Add ½ teaspoon salt, ⅛ teaspoon pepper, and a small amount of milk. Use wire whisk to blend. Heat butter in pan or skillet. Add egg mixture. Cook and stir until desired consistency. Optional: Serve with buttered toast.

Extra Helpings

1. Look up some of the animals mentioned in *It Wasn't My Fault* such as the aardvark, pygmy hippopotamus, or rabbit. Find three interesting facts about each one.
2. Think about eggs and how we use them. Make a list.
3. Write your own funny story.
4. When you make a mistake, do you take the blame? Tell someone at home.
5. Are birds the only creatures that lay eggs? Find out. Tell your family.

Books for Dessert

Heller, Ruth. *Chickens Aren't the Only Ones*. Putnam, 1981.

Hooper, Meredith. *Seven Eggs*. HarperCollins Publishers, 1985.

Peet, Bill. *The Pinkish, Purplish, Bluish Egg*. Houghton Mifflin Company, 1984.

Seuss, Dr. *Green Eggs and Ham*. Random House, 1960.

Seuss, Dr. *Horton Hatches the Egg*. Random House, 1940.

No-Cook Strawberry Jam

Jamberry
by Bruce Degen
(HarperCollins, 1983)

Before You Cook

This book is about bears who know the sheer joy of picking lots and lots of berries to eat, making them into jam, and enjoy! While they are in season, make your own no-cook jam from red, ripe strawberries.

From the Store

- strawberries
- lemon
- dry pectin
- light corn syrup
- crackers or bread, optional

From the Pantry

- sugar

Utensils to Gather

- knife
- cutting board
- measuring cup
- colander
- large bowl
- potato masher or food processor
- large mixing spoon

No-Cook Strawberry Jam (cont.)

No-Cook Strawberry Jam Recipe

- 2 quarts strawberries
- ¼ cup lemon juice
- 1 cup light corn syrup
- 1¾ to 2 oz. package dry pectin
- 4½ cups sugar

Wash, hull, and crush strawberries using either the potato masher or food processor. Place in large bowl. Add ¼ cup lemon juice and dry pectin and mix thoroughly. Continue mixing every 5 minutes for ½ hour in order to allow pectin to completely dissolve. Add light corn syrup and mix again. Slowly add sugar and continue stirring well. Refrigerate until ready to serve. Serve with toast, crackers, or bread. Mmm!

Extra Helpings

1. What is your favorite jam? Ask your friends and relatives, too. What did you find out? Make a graph of their answers.
2. What words rhyme with jam? Make a list.
3. Try writing a rhyme using words from the list you made.
4. Is jam used only on toast? Find out about different ways we might use jam.
5. Find out what kinds of conditions and soil are needed to grow strawberries and blueberries.

Books for Dessert

Hoban, Russell. *Bread and Jam for Frances*. Harper & Row, 1965.

Joosse, Barbara. *Jam Day*. Harper & Row, 1987.

Lord, John and Jane Burroway. *The Giant Jam Sandwich*. Houghton Mifflin, 1973.

McCloskey, Robert. *Blueberries for Sal*. Puffin Books, 1948.

Moore, Elaine. *Grandma's House*. Lothrop, Lee & Shepard Books, 1985.

Moore, Elaine. *Grandma's Promise*. Lothrop, Lee & Shepard Books, 1988.

Apple Crisp

Johnny Appleseed
by Steven Kellogg
(Scholastic, 1989)

Before You Cook

This is a tall tale about John Chapman, better known as "Johnny Appleseed." Born in Massachusetts in 1774, Chapman so loved apples that he wanted everyone to have an apple tree. He walked many miles through Pennsylvania, Ohio, and Indiana, telling tales and planting apple trees.

Buy or pick some apples to make this apple crisp and carry on the legend of John Chapman.

From the Store

- apples
- butter
- lemon
- optional: milk, cream, or ice cream

From the Pantry

- flour
- cinnamon
- brown sugar

Utensils to Gather

- 9" square baking pan
- two medium bowls
- spoon
- apple slicer
- measuring spoons
- measuring cup
- knife

Apple Crisp (cont.)

Apple Crisp Recipe

- 6-7 apples
- 2½ teaspoons cinnamon, divided
- 1 tablespoon lemon juice
- 1 stick butter, room temperature
- ½ cup brown sugar
- ½ cup flour
- milk, cream, or ice cream, optional

Preheat oven to 350 degrees. Slice and core apples. Place in a bowl and mix with 2 teaspoons cinnamon and lemon juice. Set aside. Meanwhile, mix together 1 stick softened butter, brown sugar, flour, and ½ teaspoon cinnamon until crumbly. Place apple slices in 9-inch square pan. Sprinkle crumbled mixture on top. Bake uncovered at 350 degrees for about 30 minutes. This dessert is especially delicious served warm with milk, cream, or vanilla ice cream.

Extra Helpings

1. Go to the library to find some other tall tales. Check out one or two and have someone at home read to you.
2. Eat an apple—they're good for you! First, estimate how many bites it will take, then count bites as you actually eat the apple.

3. Think about words that could describe apples, such as crunchy, round, red, etc. Make a list.
4. Taste several types of apples. Which type do you like best? Ask your friends and family to do this "taste test" also. What did you find out?
5. Find the states of Massachusetts, Pennsylvania, Ohio, and Indiana on a United States map.
6. Fold a piece of paper into four parts. Draw an apple tree as it would look in each season: winter, spring, summer, and fall.

Books for Dessert

Aliki. *Johnny Appleseed*. Prentice Hall, 1963.

Gibbons, Gail. *The Seasons of Arnold's Apple Tree*. Harcourt Brace Jovanovich, 1984.

LeSieg, Theo. *Ten Apples Up on Top*. Random House, 1961.

Parnall, Peter. *Apple Tree*. Macmillan, 1988.

Rockwell, Anne F., *Apples and Pumpkins*. Macmillan, 1989.

Corn Bread

Journey Cake, Ho!
by Ruth Sawyer
(Viking Press, 1953)

Before You Cook

Johnny, old man Grumble, and old woman Merry are happy with their lot in life, each performing their own chores. One night trouble begins. The animals owned by this family have various mishaps and Grumble and Merry tell Johnny he must find a new master because there will no longer be enough food to feed three. Johnny goes off with his belongings strapped to his back, including a journey cake. The journey cake falls out of his bag and Johnny runs after it, with various animals joining him in the chase. Eventually they wind up right back at the home of Grumble and Merry! The animals stay and the family is happily reunited. This cornbread recipe makes an easy and tasty journey cake.

From the Store

- cornmeal
- eggs
- butter
- milk
- canned corn

From the Pantry

- flour
- sugar
- baking powder
- salt

Utensils to Gather

- one medium bowl
- mixing spoon
- small pan
- 9" x 9" x 2" baking pan
- can opener

Corn Bread Recipe

- ¼ cup melted butter
- 1 cup corn meal
- 1 cup flour
- ¼ cup sugar
- 8 oz. can of corn
- 1 tablespoon baking powder
- ¾ teaspoon salt
- 1 egg
- 1 cup milk

Preheat oven to 425 degrees. Melt butter in small pan and cool. Add egg and milk; blend. Mix dry ingredients together in medium bowl. Add wet mixture to dry mixture, stirring only until just combined. Drain canned corn and add to batter. Pour into lightly greased 9" x 9" x 2" pan. Bake for 20-25 minutes. Serve warm with butter.

Extra Helpings

1. Try to find out why corn bread was called "journey cake." Tell your family.
2. Make a list of farm animals. Draw a picture of your favorite.
3. Draw a picture of Johnny's house. Show the setting, too. What does the "other side of Tip Top Mountain" look like? Use your imagination.
4. Design a log cabin. Use "Lincoln Logs," paper, or cardboard.
5. What are your chores at home? Make a list.

Books for Dessert

Carle, Eric. *Rooster's Off to See the World.* Picture Book Studio, 1987.

Hutchins, Pat. *Rosie's Walk.* Macmillan, 1968.

Martin, Jr., Bill and John Archambault. *Barn Dance!* Holt & Co., 1986.

McNally, Darcie. *In a Cabin in a Wood.* Dutton Children's Books, 1991.

Whole Wheat Bread

The Little Red Hen
by Paul Galdone
(Clarion Books, 1973)

Before You Cook

Working all alone, Little Red Hen has planted, raised, and harvested wheat in order to bake bread. When the other animals smell the bread's aroma, they ask the Little Red Hen to share. But the Little Red Hen refuses. The animals eventually agree that if they want to enjoy the fruit of labor, they, too, must put in effort. Enjoy the fruits of your labor when you make and eat this whole wheat bread.

From the Store

- yeast
- butter
- whole wheat flour

From the Pantry

- white flour
- salt
- brown sugar

Utensils to Gather

- measuring cups and spoons
- one small bowl
- two large bowls
- mixing spoon
- scraper
- board for kneading bread
- knife
- two 8½" x 4½" x 2½" bread pans

Whole Wheat Bread (cont.)

Whole Wheat Bread Recipe

- 1 pkg. dry yeast
- ¼ cup warm water
- 3 teaspoons salt
- 3 cups whole wheat flour
- 2½ cups hot water
- ½ cup brown sugar
- ¼ cup butter
- 5 cups white flour or as needed

Preheat oven to 375 degrees. Place dry yeast in a small bowl. Add ¼ cup warm water and allow yeast to soften and bubble. Combine hot water, brown sugar, butter, and salt in large bowl. Cool. Stir in whole wheat flour, softened yeast, and 1 cup white flour. Add enough of remaining white flour, one cup at a time, until dough is formed. Turn out onto lightly floured board and knead for 10 minutes. Shape dough into ball and place in greased bowl. Turn once to grease surface of dough. Cover and let rise in warm place for about 1½ hours. Punch down and cut in two. Shape each part into a ball. Let rest ten minutes. Shape into two loaves and place in greased bread pans. Let rise 1¼ hours. Bake 45 minutes. Cool before slicing.

Extra Helpings

1. Write a story about what you would do if you were in Little Red Hen's place. Would you share the bread or not? Why?
2. Gather together some friends. Put on a play of The Little Red Hen.
3. How many words do you know that describe bread or the bread-making process? Examples include soft, chewy, knead, etc. Make a list.
4. Write a story about a time when you were asked to help and you refused. Were you sorry later? Explain.
5. What steps do you take when you make bread? Write a sequential story.

Books for Dessert

Aesop. *Aesop's Fables*. Illustrated by Safaya Salter. Harcourt Brace & Co., 1992.

Fox, Mem. *Hattie and the Fox*. Macmillan, 1987.

Hutchins, Pat. *Rosie's Walk*. Macmillan, 1968.

Kellogg, Steven. *Chicken Little*. William Morrow & Co., 1985.

Lobel, Arnold. *Fables*. HarperCollins Publishers, 1980.

Stoeke, Janet. *A Hat for Minerva Louise*. Dutton Children's Books, 1994.

Surprise in the Middle Muffins

Little Red Riding Hood
Illustrated by Karen Schmidt
(Scholastic Inc., 1986)

Before You Cook

Little Red Riding Hood's mother gives her a basket of goodies to take to her sick grandmother and warns her not to take the path through the woods. But Little Red Riding Hood fails to heed her mother and runs into trouble— the big, bad wolf! As everyone knows, Little Red Riding Hood and Grandmother are all right in the end and enjoy the goodies in the basket after all. Read the story, then make your own basket of goodies to take to a friend.

From the Store

- juice boxes, any flavor
- strawberry jam
- eggs
- butter
- milk
- paper muffin liners

From the Pantry

- flour
- baking powder
- baking soda
- salt
- sugar
- vanilla

Utensils to Gather

- measuring cups and spoons
- two medium mixing bowls
- mixing spoon
- scraper
- small pan
- muffin tins
- hot plate

Surprise in the Middle Muffins Recipe

- 1½ cups flour
- 2 teaspoons baking powder
- ½ teaspoon salt
- ½ teaspoon baking soda
- ¼ cup sugar
- ¼ cup butter,

melted
- 2 eggs
- 1 cup milk
- ½ teaspoon vanilla
- strawberry jam

Preheat oven to 375 degrees. Place paper liners in muffin tin. Melt butter and set aside to cool. In one medium bowl, mix together dry ingredients. In another medium bowl, mix together eggs, milk, vanilla, and cooled melted butter. Add dry ingredients to wet mixture and mix until well blended. Fill each muffin cup about ¼ full. Place one spoonful of strawberry jam into each muffin, pushing down with end of spoon. Muffins will rise over the jam to make a surprise inside. Bake for 15–20 minutes. Cool before eating.

To assemble the basket of goodies:

Use a small basket or an empty plastic fruit basket with a pipe cleaner handle. Place an unfolded napkin in the basket. Put a juice box and a muffin in the basket. Tie a pretty ribbon on the handle. Give to any friend, sick or well.

Extra Helpings

1. Little Red Riding Hood did not listen carefully to her mother's warnings. What would you do if you were she? Write it down.

2. Find some facts about wolves and write down the five most interesting ones.

3. Write a new ending for the story.

Books for Dessert

Blundell, Tony. *Beware of Boys*. Greenwillow Books, 1992.

Ernst, Lisa. *Little Red Riding Hood: A New Fangled Prairie Tale*. Simon & Schuster Books for Young Readers, 1995.

Grimm Brothers. *Little Red Riding Hood*. Illustrated by Paul Galdone. McGraw-Hill, 1974.

Young, Ed. *Lon PoPo: A Red Riding Hood Story from China*. Scholastic Inc. 1989.

m&m's® Cookies

M&M's Counting Book
by Barbara McGrath
(Charlesbridge, 1994)

Before You Cook

Count from 1 to 12, learn color names, explore shapes, and practice adding and subtracting with the help of this book. When you are finished, you can eat your "math tools!" You can explore the taste of chocolate candy, too, when you bake your own cookies. Just follow the recipe on page 95.

From the Store

- m&m's® candies
- butter
- eggs
- cream of tartar

From the Pantry

- flour
- sugar
- salt
- baking soda
- cinnamon

Utensils to Gather

- measuring cups and spoons
- two medium mixing bowls
- one small bowl
- mixing spoon or hand mixer
- scraper
- cookie sheet

m&m's® Cookies Recipe

- 1½ cups flour
- 1 teaspoon cream of tartar
- ½ teaspoon baking soda
- ¼ teaspoon salt
- ½ cup butter at room temperature
- ¾ cup sugar
- 1 egg
- 1 teaspoon sugar
- 1 teaspoon cinnamon
- large bag m&m's® candies

Preheat oven to 400 degrees. Mix first four dry ingredients together and set aside. Mix together cinnamon and 1 teaspoon sugar in a small bowl and set aside. Cream together butter and ¾ cup sugar. Add eggs and dry ingredients. Mix well. Form dough into small balls, then roll in cinnamon sugar. Place on clean cookie sheet and decorate with the candies. Bake 8-10 minutes or until lightly browned but still soft. Try these cookies warm with a glass of cold milk.

Extra Helpings

1. Get a small bag of m&m's® candies. Estimate how many candies are in the bag. Open the bag and count. Were you close?

2. Make a list of the colors of candies in your small bag. Which color has the most? The least? Any ties? Any zeros?

3. Make a pattern with your candies. Have a friend continue or repeat the pattern.

4. How many ways can you make an array using 24 candies? Make a list.

5. With a friend, do some addition and subtraction problems with your candies. Write the problems that you create.

Books for Dessert

Hamm, Diane. *How Many Feet in the Bed?* Half Moon Books published by Simon & Schuster, 1994.

Karlin, Nurit. *Ten Little Bunnies*. Little Simon published by Simon & Schuster, 1994.

Pinczes, Elinor. *One Hundred Hungry Ants*. Houghton Mifflin, 1993.

Ryan, Pam. *One Hundred is a Family*. Hyperion Books for Children, 1994.

Tildes, Phyllis. *Counting on Calico*. Charlesbridge, 1995.

Wood, Jakki. *One Tortoise, Ten Wallabies*. Bradbury Press, 1994.

Cheeseburger Pie

A Medieval Feast
by Aliki
(Harper & Row, 1983)

Before You Cook

The King is going to spend a few nights at Camdenton Manor. Because the King traveled with a large party, many people would have to be fed. Preparations include cleaning, setting up tents, and gathering provisions for the great feast. As you read, you will learn about life in the Middle Ages. The book itself is also a "feast," both for reading and viewing.

You can have your own feast when you prepare and eat Cheeseburger Pie.

From the Store

- ground beef
- prepared pie crust
- onion
- garlic
- milk
- dill pickles
- cheese, Swiss or American

From the Pantry

- flour
- salt

Utensils to Gather

- 8" pie tin
- skillet or frying pan
- spoon
- small bowl
- measuring cups and spoons
- knife
- chopping board
- pie server

Cheeseburger Pie (cont.)

Cheeseburger Pie Recipe

- 1 single prepared pie crust
- 1 lb. ground beef
- ¾ cup chopped onion
- 1 clove garlic, minced
- ⅓ cup milk
- ½ teaspoon salt
- ¼ cup flour
- ⅓ cup liquid from a dill pickle jar
- ½ cup chopped dill pickles
- 2 cups grated or shredded cheese, divided

Bake prepared pie crust according to package directions, then leave oven preheated to 425 degrees. Brown ground beef in skillet or frying pan. Drain fat into small bowl and set aside. Add onion and garlic to ground beef. Cook until tender. Sprinkle salt and flour into meat mixture. Stir. Add liquid from dill pickles, dill pickles, milk, and 1 cup of the grated shredded cheese. Mix together. Spoon meat mixture into prepared pie crust and bake 15 minutes. Pull pie from oven and sprinkle remaining cup of grated or shredded cheese on top of meat. Return pie to oven for about 5 minutes longer or until crust is lightly browned and cheese on top of pie is melted. Cut into wedges to serve.

Extra Helpings

1. Look up the Middle Ages in the encyclopedia. Find five interesting facts about that time period. Write them down.

2. Get a CD or tape of medieval music. Play it for friends.

3. Go to the library. See if you can find some pictures of medieval art or of tapestries woven in the Middle Ages.

4. Look at costumes of the Middle Ages and write a story about your life if you wore such clothing.

Books for Dessert

Anderson, H. C. *The Princess and the Pea*. Illustrated by Eve Tharlet. Picture Book Studio, 1991.

Clements, Gillian. *The Truth About Castles*. Carolrhoda Books, 1990.

Cohen, Peter Zachary. *Olson's Meat Pies*. R & S Books, 1989.

Macaulay, David. *Castle*. Houghton Mifflin Co., 1977.

Millet, C. and D. *Castles*. First Discovery Books. Scholastic Inc., 1993.

Morgan, Gwyneth. *Life in a Medieval Village*. HarperCollins Publishers, 1991.

Munsch, Robert. *The Paper Bag Princess*. Annick Press Ltd., 1980.

VanWoerkom, Dorothy. *Meat Pies & Sausages: Three Tales of Fox & Wolf*. Greenwillow Books, 1976.

"Cat's Meow" Salad

Millions of Cats
by Wanda Ga'g
(Scholastic Inc., 1956)

Before You Cook

A lonely old man and woman wish for a cat to keep them company. When the old man searches for just such a cat, he comes upon so many he can hardly choose! He winds up choosing them all—hundreds and thousands and millions and billions and trillions of cats! Soon the cats began to quarrel, arguing over who is the prettiest and creating lots of noise with their fighting. When the fighting stops, only one small kitten is left. The old man and the old woman keep that kitten and help it grow into a big, beautiful cat. Whether or not you have a cat, you will lick your whiskers over this "Cat's Meow" Salad.

From the Store

- canned peach halves
- canned apricot halves
- pimento
- multi-colored curly pasta
- cheese slices
- red leaf lettuce

From the Pantry

- raisins

Utensils to Gather

- can opener
- plate
- knife (for cutting cheese)
- small pot
- hot plate

"Cat's Meow" Salad (cont.)

"Cat's Meow" Salad Recipe

- 1 large piece lettuce
- 1 canned peach half
- 1 canned apricot half
- 1 piece curly pasta
- 4 raisins
- 1 slice cheese, slivered
- 1 small piece pimento

Cook a small amount of curly pasta according to package directions. Place a piece of washed red leaf lettuce on plate. Arrange other ingredients as shown in the drawing, placing peach and apricot halves round side up and using raisins for eyes and ears, pimento for mouth, and cooked pasta for the tail. Place thinly sliced slivers of cheese on either side of apricot half to make whiskers.

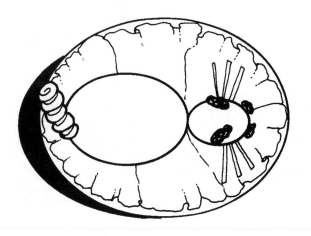

Extra Helpings

1. Find some interesting facts about cats. Tell an adult.
2. What is a billion? How many zeros does it have? How about a trillion?
3. If you were lonely, what would you do? Write a story.
4. If you have a pet, why did you get it? If you don't have a pet, which one would you like?

Books for Dessert

Birch, David. *The King's Chessboard*. Dial Books for Young Readers, 1988.

Karasz, Keiko. *Wolf's Chicken Stew*. Putnam Publishing Group, 1989.

King, Olive. *Me and My Million*. Crowell, 1979.

Schwartz, David M. *How Much Is a Million?* Scholastic Inc., 1985.

Ward, Cindy. *Cookie's Week*. Scholastic Inc., 1988.

Pita Pocket Cheese Sandwich

The Mitten
by Alvin Tresselt
(Scholastic Inc., 1964)

Before You Cook

This is but one version of an old Russian folk tale. In it, a boy loses a mitten in the snow. A mouse is the first to find the mitten and crawls inside it to keep warm. Larger and larger animals join the mouse until the mitten is very crowded. The second to last animal to come along is a bear, who pops open the seams as it tries to crawl in, but it is the last animal, a tiny cricket, that causes the mitten to completely fall apart. When the boy returns, all he finds is some yarn. Pretend a pita bread is a mitten and fill it using this simple recipe.

From the Store

- pita bread
- cheese slices
- tomato
- lettuce
- sprouts
- mayonnaise or whipped salad dressing

From the Pantry

- nothing

Utensils to Gather

- knife
- cutting board
- spreading knife

Pita Pocket Cheese Sandwich (cont.)

Pita Pocket Cheese Sandwich Recipe

- 1 piece of pita bread
- 2 slices cheese, your favorite kind
- 2 slices tomato
- 1 piece or more lettuce, chopped
- 1 serving sprouts
- 1 tablespoon mayonnaise or other whipped salad dressing

Cut pita bread in half to make two pockets. Thinly slice tomato. Wash and dry some lettuce leaves. Chop them. Open pita pockets gently. Spread with mayonnaise or whipped salad dressing. Stuff with chopped lettuce, tomato slices, and cheese slices. Top with sprouts.

Extra Helpings

1. Use your hand to trace and cut a mitten shape from construction paper. Decorate your mitten.

2. Why do you think the cricket was the one who finally caused the mitten to split apart? Write down your thoughts.

3. Read another version of this story. Compare them. Tell your family how the versions are alike and how they are different.

4. Find another folk tale. Read it yourself or have someone at home read it to you.

Books for Dessert

Brett, Jan. *The Mitten Retold*. Putnam, 1990.

Ginsburg, Mirra. *Mushroom in the Rain*. Macmillan, 1974.

Rylant, Cynthia. *The Relatives Came*. Macmillan, 1985.

Wood, Audrey. *The Napping House*. Harcourt Brace, 1984.3

Dinosaur Sandwich

Mrs. Toggle and the Dinosaur
by Robin Pulver
(Scholastic, Inc., 1991)

Before You Cook

Mrs. Toggle finds out she will have a new student in her class—a dinosaur! Can Mrs. Toggle and her students get ready in time? Read this story to find out about Mrs. Toggle's new student. Also, try making this "dinosaur" sandwich snack for an after-school treat.

From the Store

- white bread
- cheddar cheese
- slivered almonds
- small, thick pretzel sticks

From the Pantry

- peanut butter
- raisins

Utensils to Gather

- knife for cutting
- knife for spreading
- small plate

Dinosaur Sandwich (cont.)

Dinosaur Sandwich Recipe

- 1 slice bread
- 1 tablespoon peanut butter
- 8 pieces of slivered almonds
- 1 small, thick pretzel stick
- 2 raisins
- 1 triangle-shaped chunk of cheese

Cut bread in half on the diagonal. Spread peanut butter on both halves. Put halves together to form the dinosaur's body. Stick almond pieces into the peanut butter between the halves to form a "spine." Using the cheese chunk as a head, put raisins on each side for "eyes." Using the pretzel as a neck, push one end into the "head" and the other into the "body." Now you have a dinosaur sandwich!

Extra Helpings

1. Look up "dinosaurs" in an encyclopedia and draw your favorite one.
2. Create a diorama of construction paper dinosaurs and foliage inside an old shoe box.
3. What does the word "triceratops" mean? Look it up and tell an adult.
4. Some dinosaurs were plant eaters and some were meat eaters. Make a list for each type of dinosaur.
5. What was the length of your favorite dinosaur? Measure and cut a piece of string to match the dinosaur's length, then stretch the string on the ground so you can see the dinosaur's full size.

Books for Dessert

Carrick, Carolyn. *What Happened to Patrick's Dinosaurs?* Houghton Mifflin, 1988.

Cosner, Sharon. *Dinosaur Dinners.* Watts, Franklin, Inc., 1991.

Murphy, Jerry. *The Last Dinosaur.* Scholastic, Inc., 1988.

Prelutsky, Jack. *Tyrannosaurus Was a Beast.* Greenwillow Books, 1988.

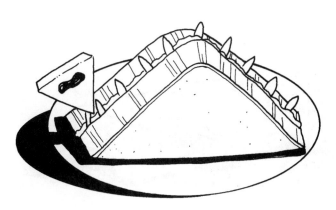

Ants on a Log

One Hundred Hungry Ants
by Elinor J. Pinczes
(Houghton Mifflin Company, 1993)

Before You Cook

One hundred hungry ants march off to a picnic. Believing they are marching too slowly, they divide into two rows of 50, then four rows of 25, and so on. By the time they get to the picnic site, all the food is gone and ninety-nine ants go after one, who cries that he isn't to blame!

Try this recipe for "Ants on a Log." The "logs" can be taken on a picnic or eaten at home. Make plenty so you won't run out!

From the Store
- celery
- cream cheese and/or peanut butter

From the Pantry
- raisins

Utensils to Gather
- knife
- cutting board
- spreading knife or spoon

Ants on a Log (cont.)

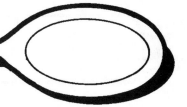

Ants on a Log Recipe

- 1 piece of celery, about 4 inches long
- 2 tablespoons cream cheese or peanut butter
- 6–8 raisins

Wash and trim celery. Cut each stalk into 2 or 3 pieces. Spread pieces with cream cheese and/or peanut butter, as desired. Place raisins in a line on top. Now you've made "ants on a log!"

Extra Helpings

1. Write a story about a time when you got blamed for something that truly wasn't your fault.
2. See if you can observe an ant farm. What do you see?
3. What if there were only 24 hungry ants? What sorts of lines could they make? Make arrays or write the number facts.
4. Sing the song "The Ants Go Marching One by One" for your family or friends.

Books for Dessert

Masaichiro, Jarby and Mitsumasa Anno. *Anno's Mysterious Multiplying Jar*. Philomel Books, 1983.

Mathews, Louise. *Bunches and Bunches of Bunnies*. Dodd Mead, 1978.

Pinczes, Elinor. *A Remainder of One*. Houghton Mifflin Company, 1995.

Williams, Vera. *A Chair for My Mother*. Greenwillow Books, 1982.

Buttermilk Pancakes

Pancakes for Breakfast
by Tomie dePaola
(Scholastic Inc., 1991)

Before You Cook

In this wordless book, a woman gets up in the morning and thinks about having pancakes for breakfast. As she prepares to make the pancakes, she discovers she is missing some key ingredients. She goes out to get them and returns home to make batter. She then churns some butter but then finds she's out of maple syrup. She goes out again to buy syrup, then returns home to discover that her dog and cat have helped themselves to the batter! She is very disappointed until, by using her sense of smell, she discovers the next door neighbors are making pancakes, too! Enjoy these buttermilk pancakes, but keep any dogs or cats away from the batter!

From the Store

- buttermilk
- butter
- eggs
- syrup

From the Pantry

- flour
- baking powder
- baking soda
- salt
- vegetable oil

Utensils to Gather

- measuring cups and spoons
- medium to large mixing bowl
- wire whisk or mixer
- frying pan or griddle
- ladle
- pancake turner or spatula
- hot plate

Buttermilk Pancakes (cont.)

Buttermilk Pancakes Recipe

- 2 cups buttermilk
- 2 eggs
- ⅛ teaspoon salt
- 1½ teaspoons baking powder
- 1 teaspoon baking soda
- 1¾ cups flour

Mix all ingredients together in bowl. Use a ladle to drop the mixture onto a hot, greased griddle or frying pan. Turn when there are bubbles all over the wet side and cook until brown. Serve with butter and syrup.

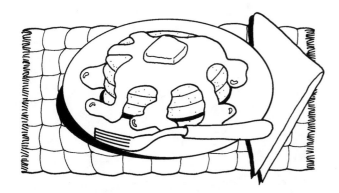

Extra Helpings

1. *Pancakes for Breakfast* is a wordless book. Write your own story to go with the pictures in this book.

2. Pancake is a compound word, that is, one word made up of two words. Do you know any other compound words? Make a list.

3. What other foods do you like to eat for breakfast? Draw a picture of your favorite breakfast. Label the foods.

4. Invite a few friends to your house for breakfast. (Be sure to check this with your family, first.) Serve pancakes with a variety of toppings including fruit, yogurt, flavored syrups, jam, or jelly.

Books for Dessert

Carle, Eric. *Pancakes, Pancakes!* Scholastic Inc., 1990.

Chalmers, Audrey. *Hundreds and Hundreds of Pancakes.* Viking, 1942.

Drucker, Malka. *Grandma's Latkes.* Harcourt Brace & Co., 1992.

Eberts, Marjorie and Margaret Gisler. *Pancakes, Crackers, and Pizza.* Children's Press, 1984.

Peanut Butter and Jelly Sandwich

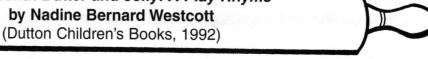

Peanut Butter and Jelly: A Play Rhyme
by Nadine Bernard Westcott
(Dutton Children's Books, 1992)

Before You Cook

This delightful book uses unusual drawings to illustrate the sequence of making a sandwich, from baking the bread, mashing the peanuts, squashing the grapes, and eating the sandwich. This easy treat is the perfect companion.

From the Store

- sliced white or wheat bread
- grape jelly

From the Pantry

- peanut butter, crunchy or smooth

Utensils to Gather

- spreading knife
- cutting knife
- cutting board

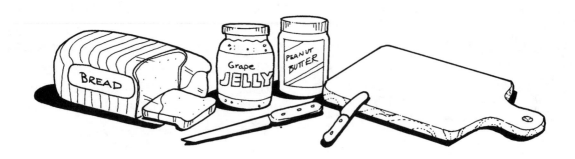

Peanut Butter and Jelly Sandwich (cont.)

Peanut Butter and Jelly Sandwich Recipe

- 2 slices bread
- 1 tablespoon peanut butter
- 1 tablespoon grape jelly

Place 2 slices of bread on cutting board. Spread peanut butter on one slice. Spread jelly on other slice. Put the two slices together to make a sandwich. Cut into fourths and eat.

Extra Helpings

1. What is your favorite sandwich? Write a story about why you like it or tell an adult.
2. Write a sequential story about the steps to use when making your favorite sandwich.
3. Draw a picture that shows things out of proportion. Tell someone older about your picture.
4. Learn the rhyme from the book. Put on a show for your friends

Books for Dessert

Delton, Judy. *Peanut Butter Pilgrims*. Dell, 1988.

Hoban, Russell. *Bread and Jam for Francis*. Harper & Row, 1986.

Lord, John and Jane Burroway. *The Giant Jam Sandwich*. Houghton Mifflin, 1990.

Palacios, Argentina. *Peanut Butter, Apple Butter, Cinnamon Toast: Food Riddles for You to Guess*. Raintree Publishers, 1990.

Robbins, Ken. *Make Me a Peanut Butter Sandwich*. Scholastic Inc., 1992.

Stutchner, Joan B. *Peanut Butter Waltz*. Firefly Books Ltd., 1990.

Walton, Sherry. *Books Are for Eating*. Dutton Children's Books, 1990.

English Muffin Pizzas

Pizza Party!
by Grace Maccarone
(Scholastic Inc., 1994)

Before You Cook

A group of children make pizza from scratch by mixing and kneading the dough, letting it rise, stretching it, spreading the sauce, and putting on the toppings. When the pizza is finished baking, the children have a pizza party.

You can create a pizza party without any fuss by making these English muffin pizzas.

From the Store

- English muffins
- jars of pizza sauce
- grated mozzarella cheese
- pepperoni
- mushrooms
- green pepper

From the Pantry

- nothing

Utensils to Gather

- large cookie sheet or pizza pan
- spatula
- knife
- cutting board

English Muffin Pizzas (cont.)

English Muffin Pizzas Recipe

- 12 English muffins, split
- two 14 oz. (400 g.) jars pizza sauce
- 1 lb. grated mozzarella cheese
- pepperoni, mushrooms, green pepper (as desired)

Preheat oven to 425 F degrees. Place English muffin halves on baking sheet or pizza pan. Spread about 1/4 cup pizza sauce on each muffin half. Sprinkle with grated cheese or place favorite toppings on before sprinkling with cheese. Bake about 10-15 minutes until cheese is melted and lightly brown.

Extra Helpings

1. Write and illustrate a story about making English muffin pizzas.
2. Where does pizza come from? You may need to go to the library to find out or ask an adult.
3. What is the weirdest kind of pizza you can think of? Write about it.

Books for Dessert

Barbour, Karen. *Little Nino's Pizzeria.* Harcourt Brace Jovanovich, 1991.

Khalsa, Dayal K. *How Pizza Came to Queens.* Crown Books for Young Readers, 1989.

Martino, Teresa. *Pizza!* Steck-Vaughn Company, 1992.

McMillan, Bruce. *Eating Fractions.* Scholastic Inc., 1991.

Pilar, Marjorie. *Pizza Man.* Crowell, 1990.

Rey, Margaret and H. A. *Curious George and the Pizza.* Houghton Mifflin Company, 1985.

Caramel Corn

The Popcorn Book
by Tomie dePaola
(Holiday House, 1978)

Before You Cook

Tony and Tina want to make popcorn. While Tony makes the popcorn on top of the stove, Tina reads aloud interesting facts about popcorn. Do you want to know who discovered popcorn, why popcorn should be stored in the refrigerator, or how many pounds of popcorn Americans eat each year? If you do, then read this book. If you want to enjoy some special popcorn, too, try this recipe for Caramel Corn.

From the Store

- popcorn (raw kernels or pre-popped)
- light corn syrup
- peanuts, optional

From the Pantry

- salt
- vanilla
- brown sugar
- baking soda
- oil, optional

Utensils to Gather

- measuring cups and spoons
- medium pot
- spoon
- large bowl
- two jelly roll pans 15" x 10" x 1" or a large roasting pan
- hot plate

Caramel Corn (cont.)

Caramel Corn Recipe

- ¾ cup unpopped popcorn kernels and ¼ cup oil for popping corn or pre-popped popcorn
  (about 7½ quarts)
- 1 cup or 2 sticks butter or margarine
- 2 cups brown sugar, packed
- ½ cup light corn syrup
- 1 teaspoon salt
- 1 teaspoon vanilla
- 1 teaspoon baking soda
- 1 cup peanuts, optional

Preheat oven to 200 degrees. If you are popping your own corn, heat oil in a large pot, then pour in popcorn. Cover with lid and shake pot on stove until all kernels have popped. Place freshly popped or pre-popped popcorn in large bowl. Melt butter in large pot and add brown sugar, light corn syrup and salt. Heat for 5 minutes, stirring occasionally. Add vanilla and baking soda. Mix thoroughly. Pour over popcorn. Add peanuts, if desired, and stir so that both popcorn and peanuts are well coated with the wet mixture. Spoon into two jelly roll pans or into large roasting pan. Bake for 1 hour, stirring every 15 minutes. Cool, then store in covered containers.

Extra Helpings

1. Think about words that rhyme with "pop." Make a list.
2. Locate some of the cities and countries named in the book on U.S. and world maps.
3. What are the three basic types of corn? Name them and tell how each is used.
4. Cut out a sheet of plain white paper so it resembles a piece of fluffy popcorn. Write words that describe popcorn on it. Invite your friends to add to the list.
5. Estimate how many popcorn kernels are in ½ cup. Count them. Was your estimate close? Did you count by twos, fives, tens, or some other number?

Books for Dessert

Asch, Frank. *Popcorn*. Parents' Magazine Press, 1979.

Greene, Ellin. *Princess Rosetta and the Popcorn Monkey*. Lothrop, Lee and Shepard, 1971.

Low, Alice. *The Popcorn Shop*. Scholastic Inc., 1993.

Thayer, Jane. *The Popcorn Dragon*. William Morrow, 1989.

Elephant Ears

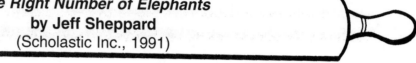

The Right Number of Elephants
by Jeff Sheppard
(Scholastic Inc., 1991)

Before You Cook

Counting backwards from 10 to 1 can be fun, especially if you use the right number of elephants to help you. Other fun situations calling for the right number of elephants include pulling a train out of a tunnel, painting a ceiling, providing shade at the beach, and racing against an unpleasant person. Try these Elephant Ears as a sweet, crisp treat.

From the Store
- butter
- milk

From the Pantry
- flour
- sugar
- baking powder
- salt
- cinnamon

Utensils to Gather
- measuring cups and spoons
- medium bowl
- pastry brush
- rolling pin
- sharp knife
- small pan
- cookie sheets
- hot plate

Elephant Ears (cont.)

Elephant Ears Recipe

- ¼ cup butter
- 1 cup flour
- 5 tablespoons sugar, divided
- ½ teaspoon baking powder
- ½ teaspoon salt
- ⅓ cup milk
- 1 teaspoon ground cinnamon
- sugar

Preheat oven to 425 degrees. Grease cookie sheet. Melt butter using small pan; allow to cool. Mix together 3 tablespoons sugar and the cinnamon in a small bowl; set aside. In medium bowl, mix together flour, 2 tablespoons sugar, baking powder and salt. Stir in milk and 3 tablespoons of melted butter into dry mixture and blend to make a dough. Sprinkle flour on a flat surface and turn out the dough. Knead about ten times, then roll it into a 9" x 5" rectangle. Brush with remaining melted butter and sprinkle with cinnamon sugar mixture. Beginning at narrow end of rectangle, spiral dough tightly. Seal ends by pinching together. Cut into 4 slices and place cut side up on cookie sheet. Pat down each slice into a 6" circle. Sprinkle with remaining sugar. Bake 8 to 10 minutes or until lightly browned.

Extra Helpings

1. Think about how you would use the "right number of elephants." Write and then illustrate your story.

2. Make your own "counting backwards" book. Begin at a number other than 10 and use your favorite animal, such as a monkey or a giraffe.

3. Think about a large area. Estimate how many elephants might cover that area. How could you check your answer? Example: How many elephants would it take to cover all the ground in your school's playground or in your town?

Books for Dessert

Crews, Donald. *Ten Black Dots*. Greenwillow Books, 1986.

Hooper, Meredith. *Seven Eggs*. HarperCollins, 1986.

LeSieg, T. *Ten Apples Up on Top*. Random House, 1961.

Mayer, Florence Cassen. *The Folk Art Counting Book*. The Colonial Williamsburg Foundation, 1992.

Perkins, A. *The Ear Book*. Random House, 1968.

Tildes, Phyllis Limbacher. *Counting on Calico*. Charlesbridge Publishing, 1995.

Wood, Jakki. *One Tortoise, Ten Wallabies*. Bradbury Press, 1994.

Mouse Salad

Seven Blind Mice
by Ed Young
(Scholastic Inc., 1993)

Before You Cook

When each of seven blind mice feel part of a "strange something" that lives by their pond, they cannot figure out what it is. In the end, the reader learns that one must see the whole in order to discover its parts, and not the other way around. Making Mouse Salad will help you remember this interesting tale. Have fun!

From the Store

- canned pear halves
- raisins
- cheese slices
- leaf lettuce
- maraschino cherries

From the Pantry

- raisins

Utensils to Gather

- can opener
- knife
- cutting board
- salad plates

Mouse Salad (cont.)

Mouse Salad Recipe

- 1 large lettuce leaf
- 1 canned pear half
- 1 slice cheese, slivered
- ½ of a maraschino cherry
- 2 raisins

Arrange ingredients on washed lettuce leaf, using the pear half for the mouse's "body," raisins for "eyes," cherry for a "nose," and cheese slivers for "whiskers" and "tail."

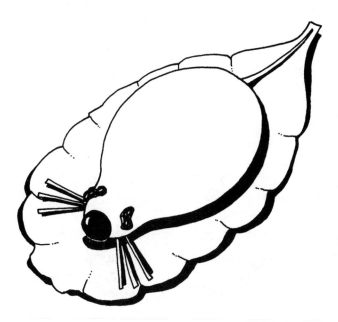

Extra Helpings

1. Write a short report about mice. Where do they like to live? What do they eat? Who are their enemies?

2. Draw part of an animal. Make the part very large and out of proportion. Ask your friends to guess what the animal is just by looking at your drawing.

3. How many weeks are in a year? How many weeks of school are there? Find out and tell your family.

5. Write a short story that has a moral. Ask an adult to help. Draw a picture to go with your story.

Books for Dessert

Kraus, Robert. *Whose Mouse Are You*? Macmillan, 1970.

Lionni, Leo. *Alexander and the Wind-Up Moose*. Alfred A. Knopf, 1969.

Lobel, Arnold. *Fables*. HarperCollins Publishers, 1980.

Lobel, Arnold. *Mouse Tales*. Harper & Row, 1972.

Steptoe, John. *The Story of Jumping Mouse*. Lothrop, Lee & Shepard, 1984.

Ward, Cindy. *Cookie's Week*. Putnam, 1988.

"Stone" Soup

Stone Soup
by Ann McGovern
(Scholastic Inc., 1986)

Before You Cook

This version of this well-known folk tale begins with a young man who is tired and hungry. He stops at a house and asks an old woman for something to eat. When the old woman says she has nothing, the young man gently tricks her into helping him make soup from a stone. The young man and old woman share the soup. Then the young man leaves, saying that the stone had not quite cooked long enough and that he would need to cook it more the following day! Follow this soup recipe and soon you'll be eating "stone" soup, too.

From the Store

- beef stew meat
- onions
- carrots
- barley
- oil
- Optional: crackers, celery, canned tomatoes, potatoes

From the Pantry

- salt
- pepper

Utensils to Gather

- measuring cup
- vegetable peeler
- large soup pot
- ladle
- chopping board and knife
- hot plate
- soup bowls
- soup spoons

Miscellaneous

- optional: large, clean, uncracked stone

"Stone" Soup Recipe

- 1 lb. beef stew meat
- 2 medium onions
- 4 large carrots
- ½ cup barley
- 6 cups water
- salt and pepper to taste
- ¼ cup oil
- crackers, optional
- vegetable choices: 1 cup sliced celery, 1 cup peeled and cubed potatoes, 1 large can tomatoes
- optional: crackers; large, clean, uncracked stone*

Peel and chop onions and carrots. Set aside. If needed, cut stew meat into small pieces, then brown in hot oil. Add chopped vegetables and water. Bring to a boil. Turn down heat and simmer until meat is tender, approximately 1 hour. Add barley and salt and pepper to taste. Cook ½ hour longer or until barley is tender. Ladle into soup bowls and serve with crackers, if desired.

*Note: If you choose to use a stone in your soup, be sure to remove it before serving. Add the stone along with the water.

Extra Helpings

1. In the story *Stone Soup*, the young man tricked the old lady. Explain how he did it to an adult.

2. Why do you think the old lady at first refused to give the young man any food? Write down your answer.

3. Ask your friends and relatives what their favorite kind of soup is. What did you find out?

4. Pretend you are going to can the soup you prepared. Design a label for "Stone Soup." What kinds of pictures will you put on the label? What other information will you include?

Books for Dessert

dePaola, Tomie. *Watch Out for the Chicken Feet in Your Soup*. Simon & Schuster, 1974.

Johnston, Tony. *The Soup Bone*. Harcourt Brace & Company, 1990.

Lobel, Arnold. *Mouse Soup*. HarperCollins Publishers, 1977.

Stewig, John W. *Stone Soup*. Holiday House, 1991.

Van Rynbach, Iris, Editor. *The Soup Stone*. Greenwillow Books, 1988.

Van Woerkom, Dorothy. *Alexandra the Rock-Eater: An Old Rumanian Tale Retold*. Alfred A. Knopf, 1978.

Deviled Eggs

Too Many Eggs: A Counting Book
by M. Christina Butler
(David R. Godine, Publisher, Inc., 1988)

Before You Cook

Mrs. Bear has to figure out how many eggs to use in Mr. Bear's birthday cake. But she has a problem doing so because she can't count! As her cake bakes, it grows so large it finally meets Mr. Bear in the woods!

If you can count to 6, you can make 12 Deviled eggs. Follow the recipe to see how it is done.

From the Store

- eggs
- mayonnaise or whipped salad dressing
- sweet pickle relish
- prepared yellow mustard
- leaf lettuce

From the Pantry

- paprika

Utensils to Gather

- bowl
- spoon
- plate
- fork
- knife
- cutting board
- pot or saucepan
- hot plate

Deviled Eggs (cont.)

Deviled Eggs Recipe

- 6 eggs
- ⅓ to ½ cup mayonnaise or whipped salad dressing
- 1/4 cup sweet pickle relish, to taste
- 1 tablespoon prepared mustard, to taste
- paprika

Hard boil the eggs. Cool under running cold water. Peel eggs, then slice each egg in half. Remove yolks and mash with fork. Mix yolks together with mayonnaise or whipped salad dressing. Add sweet pickle relish to taste and small amount of prepared mustard. Spoon mixture into egg white halves. Sprinkle tops with paprika. Arrange on lettuce leaf-lined plate and refrigerate until ready to eat.

Extra Helpings

1. Go to the library. Look up the animals mentioned in *Too Many Eggs: A Counting Book*. Find three interesting facts about each. Write them down. The animals are bear, rabbit, badger, owl, fox, squirrel, and duck.

2. How do eggs get from the farm to your house? Find out and tell an adult.

3. Why do eggs come in dozens? Try to find out.

4. Mrs. Bear cannot count. How would you teach her to do it?

5. Mrs. Bear's cake got so big it came out of the oven and continued down the hillside. Can you write a new and different ending for this story?

Books for Dessert

Heine, Helme. *The Most Wonderful Egg in the World*. Macmillan, 1983.

Hoban, Russell. *Egg Thoughts and Other Frances Songs*. HarperCollins Publishers, Inc., 1972.

Milhous, Katherine. *The Egg Tree*. Macmillan, 1971.

San Souci, Robert D. *The Talking Eggs*. Dial Books, 1989.

Wood, A. J. *Egg!* Little, Brown & Co., 1993.

Pigs in a Blanket

The True Story of the Three Little Pigs!
by Jon Scieszka
(Scholastic Inc., 1989)

Before You Cook

In this hilarious version of the classic fairy tale, "A. Wolf" claims he was framed. A. Wolf insists that the wolf in the story was only trying to borrow a cup of sugar and had sneezed, not huffed and puffed, at each little pig's door. Read the story yourself and see whether you believe A. Wolf or the third little pig.

Meanwhile, wrap your own little "pigs" in "blankets" and gobble them up.

From the Store

- cocktail hot dogs
- refrigerated crescent rolls
- ketchup and mustard, optional

From the Pantry

- nothing

Utensils to Gather

- cutting board
- knife
- toaster oven or oven
- cookie sheet
- two small dishes, optional

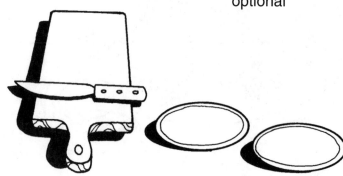

Pigs in a Blanket Recipe

- 1 tube refrigerated crescent rolls
- 1 lb. cocktail hot dogs
- ketchup
- mustard

Open crescent rolls and cut each roll in half. Wrap a cocktail hot dog with half piece of dough. Continue until you have the number of "pigs" you want. Place on cookie sheet and bake at 375 degrees for 15 minutes or until rolls are lightly browned. Before eating, dip snacks into ketchup or mustard if desired.

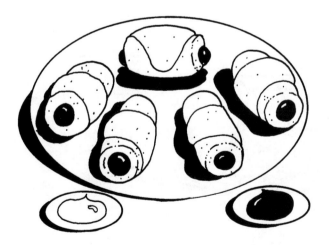

Extra Helpings

1. Find out five interesting facts about wolves or pigs. Tell an adult.

2. Use your imagination. What kind of house could be built that would be safe from the wolf? Draw a picture of it.

3. Act out the story of the three little pigs with your friends. Invite other friends to your play.

4. Do you think the wolf was really "framed"? Write your opinion and the reasons for it.

Books for Dessert

Galdone, Paul. *The Three Little Pigs.* Seabury Press, Houghton Mifflin, 1979.

Hooks, William H. *The Three Little Pigs and the Fox.* Dial Books for Young Readers, 1989.

Marshall, James. *The Three Little Pigs.* Dial Books for Young Readers, 1989.

Peet, Bill. *Chester the Worldly Pig.* Houghton Mifflin, 1978.

Zemach, Harve. *The Three Little Pigs.* An Old Story. Farrar, Strauss, & Giroux, 1989.

Fruit Salad

The Very Hungry Caterpillar
by Eric Carle
(Scholastic Inc., 1987)

Before You Cook

In this simple but charming book, a hungry caterpillar hatches from an egg and eats a different fruit each day—except Saturday, when he eats too many unusual foods and develops a stomach ache. The caterpillar recovers from his ills by eating a nice, green leaf. Then the caterpillar spins his cocoon, emerging at the end of the story as a beautiful butterfly.

You, too, can sample many different fruits when you try this recipe for Fruit Salad.

From the Store

A variety of fruits such as:

- grapes
- apples
- melon
- kiwi
- berries
- canned peaches
- canned pears
- canned fruit cocktail

From the Pantry

- plastic wrap

Utensils to Gather

- one large bowl
- one cutting board
- knife
- melon ball scoop, if available
- large spoon
- can opener

Fruit Salad (cont.)

Fruit Salad Recipe

- fresh fruits, such as those listed in "From the Store"

Example of fruit choices and amounts to use:

- 2 apples
- 1 melon
- 2 kiwi fruit
- 1/2 pound grapes
- optional: 16 oz. can fruit cocktail

You may use any other fruit that you especially like. Cut fruits into bite-sized pieces and place in large bowl. Add strained, canned fruit if desired. Mix together, cover with plastic wrap, and refrigerate until ready to serve.

Extra Helpings

1. Make your own book. Create a page for each day of the week. Draw a picture of something you like to do on each page.

2. Ask your family and friends what their favorite fruit is. What did you find out?

3. Think of foods that include fruit. Make a list.

4. Go to the library. Look up caterpillars and write down five interesting facts about them.

Books for Dessert

Carle, Eric. *The Very Busy Spider*. Philomel Books, 1984.

Fleming, Denise. *In the Tall, Tall Grass*. Holt & Company, 1991.

Gibbons, Gail. *The Monarch Butterfly*. Holiday House, 1989.

Ryder, Joanne. *Where Butterflies Grow*. Lodestar Books, 1989.

Ward, Cindy. *Cookie's Week*. Putnam, 1988.

Guacamole, Salsa, and Chips

Wednesday Is Spaghetti Day
by Maryann Cocca-Leffler
(Scholastic Inc., 1990)

Before You Cook

What do pets do when they're home alone? Make spaghetti, of course, and invite their friends over to eat it. At least, that's what Catrina the Cat does each Wednesday. But as Catrina and her friends are eating dessert, they realize that the children will be home any moment. Clean up occurs quickly, and the children never realize what happened while they were gone. Catrina, meanwhile, dreams of Thursday, the day she customarily makes guacamole.

But you don't have to wait until Thursday to make this tasty avocado dip. Make it any day, and serve it to family and friends with salsa and chips.

From the Store

- large bag of corn or tortilla chips
- jar of salsa
- ripe avocado
- lemon
- small onion
- garlic salt

From the Pantry

- plastic wrap

Utensils to Gather

- two small bowls
- one large bowl
- two spoons
- fork
- knife
- cutting board
- lemon squeezer
- small serving plates

Guacamole, Salsa, and Chips (cont.)

Guacamole, Salsa, and Chips Recipe

- 1 ripe avocado
- ½ teaspoon lemon juice
- 1 teaspoon finely chopped onion
- 1 teaspoon garlic salt
- 1 teaspoon prepared salsa
- 1 bag corn or tortilla chips

Peel and mash avocado with fork; reserve pit. Add lemon juice, finely chopped onion, garlic salt, and salsa. Mix well and scoop into bowl. Put avocado pit in center of bowl of guacamole and cover tightly with plastic wrap. The pit will prevent guacamole from turning brown. Serve guacamole dip with remaining salsa placed in a separate small bowl and large bowl of chips. Olé!

Extra Helpings

1. What is your favorite lunch? Create a menu.
2. Use your imagination. Write a story about what you think a pet might do when its family isn't home.
3. Draw a picture of a cat doing something funny.
4. Think of a food for each day of the week. Example: Monday is _____ day, Tuesday is _____, and so on.
5. Catrina's family doesn't know what has been happening at their house while they're gone. Write a story or draw a picture describing what they would find if they came home unexpectedly.

Books for Dessert

dePaola, Tomie. *Strega Nona*. Simon & Schuster Children's Books, 1979.

dePaola, Tomie. *Strega Nona's Magic Lessons*. Harcourt Brace Jovanovich, 1984.

Dr. Seuss. *The Cat in the Hat*. Random House, 1957.

Fontaine, Jan. *The Spaghetti Tree*. Talespinner, 1979.

Ga'g, Wanda. *Millions of Cats*. Putnam, 1988.

Gelman, Rita. *More Spaghetti, I Say*! Scholastic Inc., 1989.

Ward, Cindy. *Cookie's Week*. Putnam, 1988.

Tomato Soup with Oyster Crackers

Who Sank the Boat?
by Pamela Allen
(Putnam Publishing Group/Sandcastle Books, 1989)

Before You Cook

Five animals—a cow, a donkey, a sheep, a pig, and a mouse—all live at Mr. Peffer's place beside the sea. One morning, the animals decide to go for a row in the bay—and the boat sinks! Can you guess who sank the boat? Read the book so you can decide for yourself.

Try this recipe for tomato soup with oyster crackers. How many crackers will float on top of the soup?

From the Store

- canned tomato soup
- oyster crackers

From the Pantry

- nothing

Utensils to Gather

- one medium pot
- can opener
- spoon for stirring, ladle
- bowl
- soup spoon

Tomato Soup with Oyster Crackers Recipe

- 1 can tomato soup
- 1 can water
- oyster crackers

Open can of soup. Pour into pot. Slowly add one soup can of water, stirring until smooth. Cook soup until hot, approximately 4 minutes. Ladle into bowl and serve with oyster crackers floating on top.

Extra Helpings

1. Try a sink or float experiment. Fill a dish pan with water and put items into it one by one. Make separate lists of objects that sink and objects that float.

2. Use a cork, a toothpick, and a paper sail to make a boat. Better yet, make two boats and have a bathtub race.

3. Make a different kind of boat out of heavy duty aluminum foil. Put objects in the boat such as paper clips or wooden cubes. Estimate how many of these objects will fit in the boat before the boat sinks, then test your hypothesis. Was your guess close?

4. Add salt to the water in which you will float your foil boat and perform the same experiments as in number three, above. What happened?

Books for Dessert

Brett, Jan. *The Mitten*. Putnam Publishing Group, 1990.

Lillegard, Dee. *Sitting in My Box*. Dutton Children's Books, 1989.

McGovern, Ann. *Too Much Noise*. Houghton Mifflin, 1967.

Mother Goose. *The House that Jack Built*. Illustrated by Jenny Stow. Dial Books for Young Readers, 1992.

Wood, Audrey. *The Napping House*. Harcourt Brace & Co., 1984.

Special Treats for

Special Occasions

It's fun to have a party! Celebrations almost always include treats and surprises. The pages that follow contain suggestions for several different types of parties or special events. (See the list below.) Some plans have original recipes, while some plans refer to other pages in the book. The next time you have a special event coming up, turn to these pages and try an idea or two!

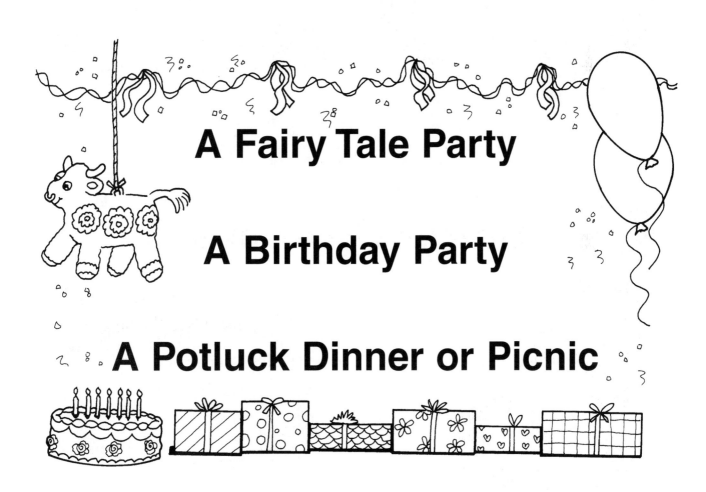

A Fairy Tale Party

A Birthday Party

A Potluck Dinner or Picnic

A Fairy Tale Party

Make yourselves into story tellers, gather in a circle, and share your favorite tales from days of yore. In addition to the party foods listed here, consider constructing a cardboard fairy tale castle by cutting and painting giant cardboard appliance boxes to look like towers. Make hats by gluing gauzy tulle fabric to paper cones or provide yellow tagboard crowns for guests to decorate with markers and glitter. Guests will also appreciate having fairy wands. These are easy to make using dowels and cardboard or plywood stars (available from crafts stores) decorated with ribbons or tinsel and spray-painted gold.

Introduce the recipes on the following pages by reading any traditional version of each fairy tale. Some interesting fairy tale versions and variations are listed below.

Briggs, Raymond. *Jim and the Beanstalk.* Coward-McCann, Inc., 1989.

Cinderella. Retold by Russell Shorto. Carol Publishing Group, 1994.

Climo, Shirley. *The Egyptian Cinderella.* HarperCollins Publishers, 1989.

Climo, Shirley. *The Korean Cinderella.* HarperCollins Publishers, 1993.

Garner, Alan, Editor. *Jack and the Beanstalk.* Doubleday, 1992.

Grimm Brothers. *Rapunzel.* Illustrated by Trina S. Hyman. Holiday House, 1989.

Grimm Brothers. *Snow White and the Seven Dwarfs*, translated and adapted by Anthea Bell. Picture Book Studio, 1991.

Perrault, Charles. *Cinderella*, retold by Barbara Karlin. Little Brown & Co., 1992.

Sage, Allison, Editor. *Rumplestiltskin.* Dial Books for Young Readers, 1990.

Steptoe, John. *Mufaro's Beautiful Daughters.* Lothrop, Lee & Shepard Books, 1987.

Cinderella's Party Punch

Cinderella

Make "Cinderella's Party Punch" to help you imagine the belle of the ball sipping a beverage with the Prince as the clock strikes midnight.

Cinderella's Party Punch

From the Store

- cranberry juice
- pineapple juice
- lemon-lime soda
- rainbow or other flavored sherbet
- lime

From the Pantry

- paper or plastic cups

Utensils to Gather

- punch bowl
- cups
- ring gelatin mold
- ladle
- cutting board
- knife

The Recipe

- 2 liters lemon-lime soda
- 48 oz. bottle cranberry juice
- 46 oz. can of pineapple juice
- 32 oz. container of sherbet
- 1 lime

Pour 4 cups of lemon-lime soda into ring gelatin mold. Freeze until firm. Pour remainder of soda into punch bowl. Add juices and mix. Remove frozen soda from ring mold and place in punch bowl. Float spoonfuls of sherbet on top. Garnish with thin slices of lime. Ladle into cups to serve.

Rapunzel's Angel Hair Pasta

Rapunzel

"Rapunzel, Rapunzel, let down your hair," the Prince called to the beautiful maiden he had spied in the witch's tower. You may not have Rapunzel's long, golden tresses, but you can enjoy "Rapunzel's Angel Hair Pasta."

Rapunzel's Angel Hair Pasta

From the Store

- angel hair pasta
- butter
- jar or can of spaghetti sauce
- grated Parmesan cheese

From the Pantry

- nothing

Utensils to Gather

- medium pot
- colander or strainer
- plates and forks

The Recipe

- 1 lb. angel hair pasta
- ½ stick butter
- 1 medium jar or can of prepared spaghetti sauce
- 8 oz. grated Parmesan cheese

Cook pasta according to package directions. Heat spaghetti sauce. Drain pasta in colander. Place pasta back into pot and toss with butter. Place serving of pasta on a plate, top with heated sauce, and serve with grated Parmesan cheese.

Jack's Three Bean Salad

Jack and the Beanstalk

Jack's mother was none too happy when her son traded their cow, Milky White, for a handful of magic beans. Little did she know that the beans would grow into a huge stalk that would lead Jack to the giant's castle full of riches. The following recipe is a tasty reminder of Jack's great adventure.

Jack's Three Bean Salad

From the Store

- red kidney beans
- sliced green beans
- sliced wax beans
- Italian salad dressing
- green onions

From the Pantry

- nothing

Utensils to Gather

- one large bowl
- spoon
- cutting board
- knife
- strainer
- can opener

The Recipe

- 15 oz. can of kidney beans
- 15 oz. can of green beans
- 15 oz. can of wax beans
- 18 oz. bottle of Italian salad dressing
- 2 green onions

Open the three cans of beans. Drain liquid using strainer. Place drained beans in bowl. Chop green onions. Add to bowl together with enough Italian dressing to moisten.

Snow White's Ice Cream Sundaes with Seven Toppings

Snow White and the Seven Dwarfs

"Mirror, mirror, on the wall, who's the fairest one of all?" Everybody knows it's Snow White, of course. Snow White may have had the burdensome task of tending house for seven dwarves, but even she and this group of laborers treated themselves to ice cream sundaes every once in awhile.

Snow White's Ice Cream Sundaes with Seven Toppings

From the Store

- vanilla ice cream
- maraschino cherries
- bananas
- chopped peanuts or peanut halves
- chocolate syrup
- butterscotch topping
- candy sprinkles
- chocolate sandwich cookies

From the Pantry

- nothing

Utensils to Gather

- medium plastic bag
- rolling pin
- serving spoon or ice cream scoop
- bowls for sundaes
- seven small bowls
- seven spoons

The Recipe

- ½ gallon vanilla ice cream
- 1 package chocolate sandwich cookies
- 1 jar maraschino cherries
- 2 bananas
- 1 jar peanuts, chopped or halved
- 1 bottle chocolate syrup
- 1 jar butterscotch topping
- 1 container candy sprinkles

Place cookies in plastic bag. Crush with rolling pin. Peel and slice bananas. Place toppings in seven separate dishes. Scoop ice cream into bowls for eating. Serve with choice of toppings.

Gingerbread Man Cookies

The Gingerbread Man

Children will enjoy decorating and eating these gingerbread cookies, which are a favorite treat all across Europe and in the United States, as well.

Gingerbread Man Cookies

From the Store

- decorator's icing
- butter or margarine

From the Pantry

- flour
- dark brown sugar
- ground ginger
- ground cinnamon

Utensils to Gather

- rolling pin
- mixing bowl
- gingerbread man cookie cutter
- cookie sheet
- mixing spoon
- measuring cups and spoons

The Recipe

- 2 ¼ cups flour
- ½ cup butter or margarine
- 10 tablespoons dark brown sugar
- 2 teaspoons ground ginger
- decorator's icing
- water

Put flour and spices into mixing bowl and mix in the butter until mixture resembles fine bread crumbs. Stir in the sugar, using a little water, and mix to a firm dough. Roll dough out on a lightly floured board to about ¼ inch thick, and use a gingerbread man cutter to cut out cookies. Place on a greased cookie sheet and bake at 325 degrees for about 15 to 20 minutes. Cool on a wire rack. Add faces and buttons with decorator's icing.

Always Room for Shortbread

Always Room for One More

Everyone who comes to this cozy home on the heather is invited in. The house becomes crowded and shortly a new house must be built. In celebration of the completion of the house, children can imagine that this Scottish shortbread might have been served and enjoyed by all.

Always Room for Shortbread

From the Store

- butter

From the Pantry

- sugar
- all purpose flour
- salt
- baking powder

Utensils to Gather

- sifter
- cookie sheet
- mixing spoon
- electric or hand mixer
- knife
- spatula
- measuring cups and spoons

The Recipe

- 1 cup butter
- $\frac{1}{2}$ cup plus 2 tablespoons sugar
- 2 cups sifted all purpose flour
- $\frac{1}{4}$ teaspoon salt
- $\frac{1}{4}$ teaspoon baking powder

Beat butter until light and creamy. Beat in $\frac{1}{2}$ cup of sugar. Sift the flour, salt, and baking powder together and fold into butter mixture. Place dough on a cookie sheet and pat it into a rectangle, $\frac{1}{2}$" thick and approximately 4"x10" in size. Sprinkle remaining sugar over the top and bake shortbread in the center of a preheated 350 degree Fahrenheit oven for 15 minutes until edges are lightly browned. Cut into bars and serve. (Serves 20)

A Birthday Party

It's time for a birthday party! Have you thought about a theme for your party? What kind of food and games will you have? No matter what kind of birthday party you have planned, you and your child are sure to have fun preparing the goodies on the following pages.

Set the stage with the birthday book, *Happy Birthday, Jessie Bear!* by Nancy White Carlstrom (Macmillan Publishing Company, 1994). Decorations, balloons, gifts, and a cake with candles are all part of Jessie Bear's birthday.

Additional books you and your children will enjoy include the following:

Craig, Helen. *Angelina's Birthday Surprise*. Crown Books for Young Readers, 1989.

Hest, Amy. *Nana's Birthday Party*. Morrow Junior Books, 1993.

Lakin, Patricia. *Don't Forget*. Tambourine Books, 1994.

Polacco, Patricia. *Thundercake*. Philomel Books, 1990.

Powell, Polly. *Just Dessert*. Harcourt Brace & Company, 1996.

Here are additional ideas to make your party a success:

1. Create an invitation. Think about the information you want to include. How will you decorate it?

2. Think of some games to play at the party.

3. Create some "goodie" bags. What will you put in them?

4. Practice some songs that you would like to sing at the party.

5. Make party hats. Materials and directions can be found on the following pages.

Make a Party Hat!

Material

- for each small child: two 8½" x 14" sheets of paper (any color or white)
- for each older child or adult: two 11" x 17" sheets of paper (any color or white)
- paper or fabric scraps
- wrapping paper scraps
- buttons, sequins, beads
- ribbon in various colors
- gift-wrapping bows
- crayons and markers
- glue
- clear tape
- scissors

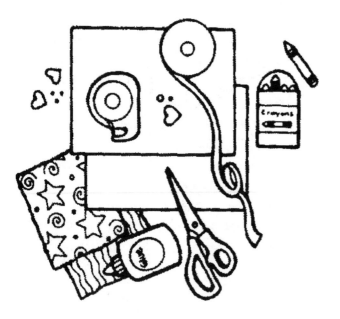

Directions

1. Take the two pieces of paper and tape them side by side down the entire length of their long edge.

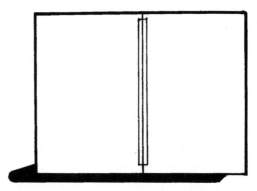

2. Fold the paper in half along the taped edge. The tape should be inside the fold.

3. Fold the paper in half again, as shown.

Make a Party Hat! *(cont.)*

4. Open the fold. Fold the top left and right corners down to meet at the center fold.

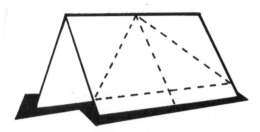

5. Fold up the bottom flap on this side and on the reverse side.

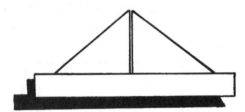

6. Pull the center front and the center back out and away from each other. Tuck one flap corner behind the other flap corner on both sides. You now have a diamond shape.

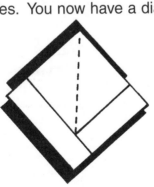

7. Fold the bottom two corners up one quarter of the entire length of the hat.

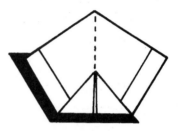

8. Pull the new center front and center back out and away from each other. You now have a pointed party hat with an eight-sided base.

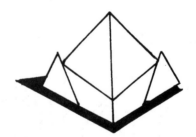

9. Decorate as desired!

Happy Birthday Pizza

Pizza

Traditional pizza is always welcomed at children's birthday parties, but this cookie dough pizza recipe is sure to be a new favorite at any party!

Happy Birthday Pizza

From the Store

- refrigerated cookie dough
- cream cheese
- sweetened condensed milk (regular, low- or non-fat)
- frozen orange juice concentrate
- toppings such as fresh or canned fruit, crushed candy bars, gummy candies, chopped nuts, or toasted coconut

From the Pantry

- vanilla

Utensils to Gather

- 14 inch pizza pan
- measuring cups
- measuring spoons
- bowl
- hand mixer
- knife, forks, spoons
- plates
- serving spatula

The Recipe

20 oz. package refrigerated cookie dough, any kind

14 oz. can sweetened condensed milk

1/2 cup frozen orange juice concentrate, defrosted

1 teaspoon vanilla

assorted toppings (see "From the Store.")

Preheat oven to 350 degrees. Press cookie dough onto lightly greased 14-inch pizza pan, forming a rim around the edge. Bake for 12-15 minutes or until lightly browned. Cool. In bowl beat cream cheese with sweetened condensed milk. Stir in orange juice concentrate and vanilla. Chill. When ready to serve, spread cream cheese mixture over cookie dough "crust." Top as desired, using suggestions given. Slice into wedges to serve.

Rich Chocolate Ice Cream

Ice Cream

This is a unique recipe for ice cream because each person can make his or her own individual portion. And the clean-up is great, too, because the ice cream can be eaten straight out of the bag!

Rich Chocolate Ice Cream

From the Store

- milk
- instant hot cocoa mix

From the Pantry

- pint-size resealable plastic bags
- gallon-size resealable plastic bags
- salt
- ice cubes

The Recipe

- 1 pint-size resealable plastic bag
- 1 gallon-size resealable plastic bag
- ½ cup milk
- 1 tablespoon instant hot cocoa mix
- 6 tablespoons regular table salt
- ice cubes

Put milk and cocoa powder in pint size bag. Seal well. Half fill the gallon size bag with ice cubes and add salt. Put the small bag inside the large bag and seal the large bag well. Shake bags about five minutes or until ice cream forms. Wipe salty water from top of small bag. Open, eat, enjoy!

Note: Ice cream will be "soft serve" style.

Birthday Party Extras

Here are two "in a pinch" ideas that will come in handy for your birthday party menu.

Quick Cake Icing

You will need the following ingredients:

- 1 pound box of confectioner's sugar
- 1 stick of margarine, softened
- enough milk to thin
- food coloring, as desired

Use a fork to blend the sugar and softened margarine. Slowly add milk until the icing is a spreading consistency. Use food coloring to tint.

Creative Clown Cookies

These cookies can be done in no time at all, and both you and your children will enjoy creating your own special clowns.

You will need the following ingredients.

- purchased oatmeal or sugar cookies
- icing (purchased or made using the Quick Cake Icing recipe)
- any or all of these ingredients: small candies, chocolate chips, marshmallows, coconut flakes, dried fruit sheets

Use the icing as "glue" to attach small candies, chocolate chips, or marshmallows to the cookies. If desired, tint coconut for hair and make a hat from thin dried fruit sheets cut into triangles.

A Potluck Dinner or Picnic

For a Potluck Dinner

Whether you are planning a pot luck dinner for a school group or for the family, kick off your cooking with *A Pot Luck Dinner*, by Anne Shelby (Orchard Books, 1994). In this story, Alpha and Betty set their table for thirty-one friends. Each friend brings a dish that begins with the same letter as their name.

Why not invite some of your friends to an "alphabet" pot luck? Ask them to bring a dish that begins with the same letter as their name. Some ideas are:

- Ben could bring a beef dish or broccoli.
- Don could bring donuts or dumplings.
- Lee could bring lemonade or lasagna.
- Have your friends bring copies of the recipe of the foods they bring to share so that everyone can try making them on their own at home.

In addition to the literature selections on the following pages, here are some books you and your children will also enjoy:

Davoll, Barbara. *Potluck Supper*. Victor Books, 1988.

Soto, Gary. *Chato's Kitchen*. G. P. Putnam's Sons, 1995.

Swanson, Patsy. *Potluck Adventures of Mrs. Marmalade*: A Children's Cookbook. Sunbelt Media, 1989.

Tobias, Tobi. *Pot Luck*. Lothrop, 1993.

For a Picnic

Picnics can be elaborate and planned, or impromptu and potluck. Whatever the motivation for a picnic, the idea is to have fun! The book selections and recipes on the following pages will help you get started.

Surprise Lunch

The Lunch Box Surprise
by Grace Maccarone
(Scholastic Inc./Cartwheel Books, 1995)

Before You Cook

Sam's mom forgot to make his lunch. His friends help him out by sharing a little of their lunch with him. He winds up having the best lunch of all!

Carry on the idea by making two lunches, including this delicious recipe for tuna salad, one for you, one for a friend. But don't tell your friend what you are bringing; let that be a surprise. Then ask your friend to make a surprise lunch for you later in the week.

From the Store

- tuna packed in water
- bread
- green onions
- mayonnaise or whipped salad dressing
- bag baby carrots
- chips, any variety
- cookies, any variety
- apples, any variety
- juice boxes, any variety

From the Pantry

- nothing

Utensils to Gather

- can opener
- knife
- cutting board
- glass
- plate
- small bowl
- paper sack

Surprise Lunch

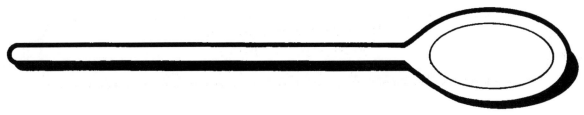

Surprise Lunch Recipe

The following ingredients make two lunches.

- 2 slices bread
- 2 green onions
- 3 tablespoons mayonnaise or whipped salad dressing
- 4 baby carrots
- 1 serving chips
- 1 apple
- 2 cookies
- 1 juice box

Open tuna and drain thoroughly. Chop green onions. Mix tuna, green onions, and mayonnaise together in a small bowl. Serve tuna salad as a sandwich on two slices of bread. Pack the sandwich and all other items in a paper sack.

Extra Helpings

1. What is your favorite school lunch? Make a menu.

2. Do you like to buy lunch at school or take a sack lunch? Tell your family which you like best.

3. What would you do if your friend or classmate forgot his or her lunch?

4. What time do you usually eat lunch? Make a clock face using a paper plate, black construction paper hands, and a brad. Show the time you eat lunch, and breakfast and dinner, too.

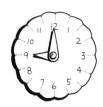

Books for Dessert

Fleming, Denise. *Lunch.* Henry Holt, 1992.

Lasky, Kathryn. *Lunch Bunnies.* Little, Brown & Co., 1993.

Lobel, Arnold. *Frog and Toad are Friends.* HarperCollins, 1970.

Lobel, Arnold. *Frog and Toad Together.* HarperCollins, 1972.

Sharmat, Marjorie. *The 329th Friend.* Macmillan, 1992.

A Picnic Lunch or Supper

The Teddy Bears' Picnic
by Jimmy Kennedy
(Green Tiger Press, 1983)

Before You Cook

"Teddy bears" go on a picnic—really children dressed up in bear costumes. There is delicious food, games to be played, and a good time for all.

From the Store

- See each recipe for ingredients.

From the Pantry

- See each recipe for staples.

Utensils to Gather

- picnic basket or cooler
- red and white checkered tablecloth
- gallon thermos jug
- blanket
- paper plates
- plastic forks, spoons, knives
- paper napkins

A Picnic Lunch or Supper (cont.)

A Picnic Lunch or Supper Recipe

Make each item, following directions given in the book. Pack in picnic basket or cooler. Take to a lovely outdoor spot and enjoy with several friends or your parent(s).

Add to your picnic by gathering a few goodies from recipes found on other pages in this book. Here are some suggestions:

- Tuna Salad Sandwiches (*The Lunch Box Surprise*)
- Zesty Pasta Salad (*Daddy Makes the Best Spaghetti*)
- Ants on a Log (*One Hundred Hungry Ants*)
- m&m's® Cookies (*M&M's Counting Book*)
- Cinderella's Party Punch (*A Fairy Tale Party*)

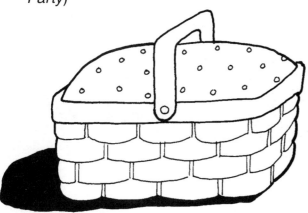

Extra Helpings

1. Tell someone older about a picnic you've been to. Did you enjoy it? Why?
2. Think of some games to play after the meal.
3. Create an invitation to the picnic. Send it to your friends. You can provide all the food or make the picnic potluck.
4. Do you want to bring some sports equipment to the picnic, such as a ball and bat? Make a list.

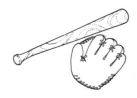

Books for Dessert

Brown, Ruth. *The Picnic*. Dutton Children's Books, 1993.

Kasza, Keiko. *Pig's Picnic*. Putnam Publishing Group, 1992.

McCully, Emily A. *Picnic*. HarperCollins Children's Books, 1984.

Mahey, Margaret. *Rattlebang Picnic*. Dial Books for Young Readers, 1994.

Miranda, Anne. *Pignic*. Boyds Mills Press, 1996.

Palacco, Patricia. *Picnic at Mudsock Meadow*. G. P. Putnam's Sons, 1992.

An "Extra Helping" of Ideas

Letters to Send Home

Dear Parent or Guardian,

This year, after reading a literature selection as a group activity, we will be preparing a recipe related to the book. *Simple Cooking Fun* will provide valuable instruction in nutrition, the pleasure of tasting different foods, and the fun of cooking. It will also give children opportunities to interact with real life extensions in reading and language arts, math, science, social studies, and social skills.

Since the children will be eating a variety of foods, I need to be informed of any allergies or other dietary restrictions.

We are accepting donations of cooking utensils and appliances as well as food staples such as sugar, flour, cooking oil, and so on. We would appreciate any kitchen extras you might be willing to send to our classroom cooking center.

Please cut out the box below and return it as soon as possible so that a successful cooking and eating experience can be provided for your child.

Thank you for your help!
Sincerely,

_____

Name of child _____

Telephone Number _____

❏ My child DOES NOT have allergies or other dietary restrictions.

❏ My child DOES have allergies or other dietary restrictions as follows:

_____

_____

❏ I can donate the following item(s) to the cooking center:

_____

_____

_____

A Trip to the Supermarket

Cooking can begin at the supermarket. In fact, each time you go to the market, you can help your child develop skills in math and reading. Don't forget a lesson in culture as you march down the international foods aisle, or an introduction to economics as you study food distribution or pricing.

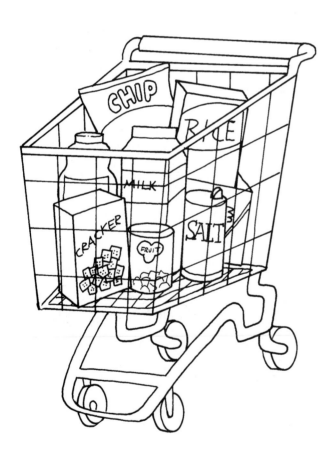

Before You Cook with Your Child

Choose one recipe from the previous pages. Create a complete list, leaving space for writing in the price of each item.

Estimate how much money you will need in order to buy the ingredients. (A sample has been provided for you.) Whether or not you will be going as part of a group, contact the store manager to see if he or she will be available to answer questions.

Some questions which you might ask are:
- When are foods delivered?
- How do foods get onto the shelves?
- Who cleans the store?
- When does it get cleaned and how often?
- How do you decide what to buy and how much to get?
- How do the checkout people learn to do their job?
- Who decides what goes on sale each week?

Solicit other questions from children. Be sure to discuss expectations for good manners, behavior, and safety while in the store.

At the Store

Think about and discuss the following questions:

- Look for unusual items in the produce section. Can anyone name them?
- Why does the produce department have scales?
- Does the store have live fish? If so, why are they kept in water?
- Can you tell if the store has a bakery just by using your nose? Why?
- Why do the freezers have glass doors?
- Are there machines for shoppers to use at the supermarket? If so, what do they do?
- Does the checkout area have talking cash registers? How do you think they work?
- Does the supermarket use computers? If so, for what jobs?

- Why do you think items are arranged the way they are in the store?
- Can any words be read from the signs in the food aisles or the directions on a box or container of food?
- Why are grocery bags packed with heavier items on the bottom?
- Look for one type of food in several forms such as fresh apples, applesauce, apple coffee cake, apple chips, taffy apples, apple juice, apple cider, apple pie, and so forth.
- Think about colors on food packaging. Which colors do you see most often? Why do you think that happens?

Supermarket Shopping List and Budget

What items do you need to buy? How much do you have to spend? These are important questions to think about before and while you are shopping. Fill out the shopping list below. After you have collected the items, write the total cost of the items you listed.

Items we will need: Price

1. _____   _____

2. _____   _____

3. _____   _____

4. _____   _____

5. _____   _____

6. _____   _____

7. _____   _____

8. _____   _____

9. _____   _____

10. _____   _____

Total cost: _____

After the Trip

Whether you are in a classroom, as part of a community group, or working with your child at home, you can continue the supermarket experience after your visit as well. Try some of the following ideas:

1. Discuss how much the items on the shopping list actually cost. Compare that to the pre-trip estimate.

2. Make a map of the supermarket. Discuss which foods go in the dairy section, produce, freezer, and so forth. Have children cut out pictures of foods from magazines, paste them on cards, and place them in the correct section of the supermarket map. Velcro® dots attached to the food picture card and the map would be helpful.

3. Make a "Where Did It Come From?" chart. Create categories such as ocean and lake, land, and animals. List foods under each category as children respond. Food picture cards could be used for this activity also.

4. Discuss how much money it takes to feed a family for one week. Have children use a calculator to figure out how much a month's worth, then a year's worth, of food would cost. They will probably be surprised at how much money it takes to feed a family!

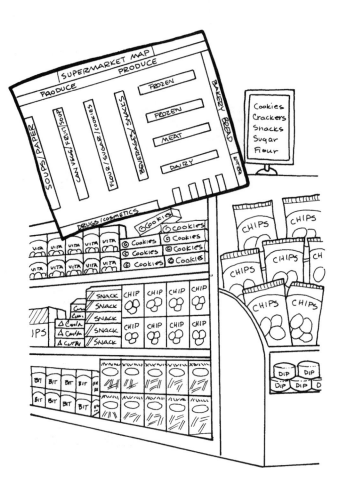

Books, Books, and More Books!

Literature Bibliography

Aliki. *A Medieval Feast*. Harper and Row, 1983.

Allen, Pamela. *Who Sank the Boat?* Putnam Publishing Group/Sandcastle Books, 1989.

Blegvad, Lenore. *Anna Banana and Me*. Simon & Schuster Children's Books, 1987.

Butler, M. Christina. *Too Many Eggs: A Counting Book*. David R. Godine, Publisher, Inc., 1988.

Carle, Eric. *The Grouchy Ladybug*. HarperCollins, 1977.

_____. *The Very Hungry Caterpillar*. Scholastic, Inc., 1987.

Carlstrom, Nancy White. *Happy Birthday, Jessie Bear!* Macmillan Publishing Co., 1994.

Christelow, Eileen. *Five Hungry Monkeys Jumping on the Bed*. Clarion Books, 1989.

Cocca-Leffler, Maryann. *Wednesday is Spaghetti Day*. Scholastic, Inc., 1990.

Day, Alexandra. *Frank and Ernest*. Scholastic, Inc., 1991.

Degen, Bruce. *Jamberry*. Harper and Row Publishers, Inc., 1983.

dePaola, Tomie. *The Cloud Book*. Scholastic, Inc., 1975.

_____. *Pancakes for Breakfast*. Harcourt Brace Jovanovich, Inc., 1978.

_____. *The Popcorn Book*. Scholastic Books, 1978.

Dooley, Norah. *Everybody Cooks Rice*. Carolrhoda Books, Inc., 1991.

Ehlert, Lois. *Eating the Alphabet*. Harcourt Brace and Co., 1989.

_____ . *Growing Vegetable Soup*. Harcourt Brace Jovanovich, Inc., 1987.

Friedman, Aileen. *A Cloak for the Dreamer*. Scholastic, Inc., 1995.

Ga'g, Wanda. *Millions of Cats*. Putnam Publishing Group, 1977.

Galdone, Paul. *The Little Red Hen*. Clarion Books, 1973.

George, Jean C. *The First Thanksgiving*. Philomel Books, 1993.

Hines, Anna G. *Daddy Makes the Best Spaghetti*. Clarion Books, 1986.

Hutchins, Pat. *The Doorbell Rang*. William Morrow and Company, Inc., 1986.

Kellogg, Steven. *Johnny Appleseed*. William Morrow and Company, Inc., 1988.

Kennedy, Jimmy. *The Teddy Bears' Picnic*. Green Tiger Press, 1983.

Kroll, Steven. *The Biggest Pumpkin Ever*. Holiday House, 1984.

Leodhas, Sorche Nic. *Always Room for One More*. Henry Holt, 1965.

Lester, Helen. *It Wasn't My Fault*. Houghton Mifflin, 1985.

Lionni, Leo. *Inch by Inch*. William Morrow and Company, Inc., 1994.

Lord, John Vernon. *The Giant Jam Sandwich*. Houghton Mifflin, 1987.

Mathews, Louise. *Gator Pie*. Sundance Publishing, 1995.

McCloskey, Robert. *Blueberries for Sal*. Puffin Books, 1976.

McGovern, Ann. *Stone Soup*. Scholastic, Inc., 1986.

McGrath, Barbara B. *The M&M's Counting Book*. Charlesbridge Publishing, 1994.

Maccarone, Grace. *The Lunch Box Surprise*. Scholastic Inc./Cartwheel Books, 1995.

_____. *Pizza Party!* Scholastic, Inc., 1994.

Marshall, James. *Goldilocks and the Three Bears*. Dial Books for Young Readers, 1988.

Martin, Bill Jr. and John Archambault. *Chicka Chicka Boom Boom*. Simon and Schuster Books for Young Readers, 1989.

Morris, Ann. *Bread, Bread, Bread.* Lothrop, Lee and Shepard Books, 1989.

Numeroff, Laura J. *If You Give a Moose a Muffin.* HarperCollins Publishers, 1991.

Pinczes, Elinor J. *One Hundred Hungry Ants.* Houghton Mifflin Company, 1993.

Pulver, Robin. *Mrs. Toggle and the Dinosaur.* Scholastic Inc., 1991.

Rey, Margaret and H. A. *Curious George and the Pizza.* Houghton Mifflin Company, 1985.

Rockwell, Anne. *Apples and Pumpkins.* Macmillan Publishing Company, 1989.

Sawyer, Ruth. *Journey Cake, Ho!* Puffin Books, 1978.

Schmidt, Karen (illustrator). *Little Red Riding Hood.* Scholastic, Inc., 1986.

Scieszka, Jon. *The True Story of the Three Little Pigs.* Viking Penguin, 1989.

Sharmat, Mitchell. *Gregory, the Terrible Eater.* Four Winds Press, 1980.

Shelby, Anne. *Potluck.* Orchard Books, 1994.

Sheppard, Jeff. *The Right Number of Elephants.* HarperCollins, 1991.

Slepian, Jan and Ann Seidler. *The Hungry Thing.* Scholastic, Inc., 1988.

Tompert, Ann. *Grandfather Tang's Story.* Crown Publishers, Inc., 1990.

Tresselt, Alvin. *The Mitten.* William Morrow and Company, Inc., 1989.

Viorst, Judith. *Alexander and the Terrible, Horrible, No Good, Very Bad Day.* Macmillan Publishing Company, 1972.

Waber, Bernard. *Ira Sleeps Over.* Houghton Mifflin, 1972.

Westcott, Nadine B. (illustrator). *Peanut Butter and Jelly, A Play Rhyme.* Dutton Children's Books, 1992.

Young, Ed. *Seven Blind Mice.* Philomel Books, 1992.

Additional Bibliography

Adoff, Arnold. *Chocolate Dreams*. Lothrop, Lee & Shepard Books, 1989.

Adoff, Arnold. *Eats Poems*. Lothrop, Lee & Shepard Books, 1979.

Bell, Louise Price. *Kitchen Fun*. Derrydale, 1988.

Cole, William, poems selected by. *Poem Stew*. HarperCollins Children's Books, 1983.

Fergus, Mary Pat. *Kids Can Cook*. Rigby, 1990.

Fleming, Denise. *Lunch*. Henry Holt & Co., 1992.

Joslin, Sesyle. *What Do you Say, Dear?* HarperCollins Children's Books, 1986.

Lillegard, Dee. *Do Not Feed the Table*. Doubleday Books for Young Readers, 1993.

McMillan, Bruce. *Eating Fractions*. Scholastic Inc., 1991.

Tobias, Tobi. *Pot Luck*. Lothrop, 1993.

Westcott, Nadine B. *Never Take a Pig to Lunch and Other Poems About the Fun of Eating*. Orchard Books Watts, 1994.